JAPAN-ease
GRAMMAR

JAPAN-ease GRAMMAR
CONJUGATION CHARTS
FOR VERBS, ADJECTIVES, AND COPULAS

TIFFANY PIERSON

Edited by
Ben Frenchman

FIRST EDITION

Copyright © 2013 by Tiffany Pierson.

All rights reserved. No part of this publication may be reproduced or distributed in any printed or electronic form without prior written permission of the author.

Published in Seattle, Washington in the United States by International Solutions Product Development.

Interior design by Rachel Hegarty

Library of Congress Control Number: 2013917559

Paperback ISBN 978-0-9860591-0-0
PDF eBook ISBN 978-0-9860591-1-7

The author respectfully acknowledges
Mai Hayano and Hideki Watanabe
for assisting with the author's
Japanese grammar research.

TABLE OF CONTENTS

PREFACE .... **XI**

**INTRODUCTION TO DIFFERENCES
BETWEEN JAPANESE AND ENGLISH** .... **XIII**

ADJECTIVES **1**
い-Adjectives 1
 Dictionary Form versus Stem, 1
 Conjugation Formula Charts, 2
 Exceptional い-Adjective いい, 6
 Example Sentence Charts, 6
 Conditional い-Adjectives, 8
 Continuative い-Adjectives, 10
 Obligation い-Adjectives, 11
な-Adjectives 12
 Dictionary Form versus Stem, 12
 な-Adjective Conjugation Formulas, 12
Adjectives, Hiragana, and Katakana 12
Noun Form 13

vii

ADVERBS ... 15
Formula Chart ... 15
Adverb Endings ... 15
Adverb Placement ... 16

COPULAS ... 17
Copulas and Nouns ... 17
Copulas and な-Adjectives ... 17
Emphasizing は ... 18
Beginnings では and じゃ ... 18
Colloquial Conditional Copulas ... 19
Copula Charts ... 19
Example Sentence Charts ... 22
Conditional Copulas ... 24
Continuative Copulas ... 25
Obligation Copulas ... 26
ある-Copulas ... 27

VERBS ... 29
Bases ... 29
    う-*Verbs*, 30
        Exceptional Verb いく, 32
    る-*Verbs*, 32
    Irregular Verbs, 33
Verb Stems and Kanji ... 33
Conjugation Formula Charts ... 35
Example Sentence Charts ... 40
Conditional Verbs ... 42
Continuative Verbs ... 43
Volitional Verbs ... 45

Obligation Verbs 46
Basic Verbs 47
Exceptional Verb ある 47
Advanced Conjugations 49
Advanced Conjugations and Particle Use 51
Stem + られる Formula 52

VERB AUXILIARIES 55

RELATIVE CLAUSES 59

Relative Clauses with a Modifying Verb 59
Relative Clauses with a Modifying い-Adjective 60
Relative Clauses with a Modifying な-Adjective 60
Relative Clauses with the Modifying
 い-Adjective おおきい, おかしい, or ちいさい 61
Relative Clauses with a Modifying Noun 62
Relative Clauses with a Modifying Informal
 Obligation Form of a Verb, Adjective, or Copula 63
Extended Relative Clauses 64

NOMINALIZERS の AND こと 67

Other Function of の and こと 68

APPENDIX A:
PARTICLES 69

Particle Chart 70
Topic Particle は and Subject Particle が 74
Direct Object Particle を, Transitive Verbs,
 and Intransitive Verbs 77

Indirect Object Particle に..78
Purpose Particle に...80
Direction Particle へ..80
Modifying Particle の..80
Verbal Question Mark Particles か and の...81
Softener Particle の..82
Dialogue and Thoughts Particle と..82
Conditional Particle と..84
Additional Noun Particle も...85
Quantity Particle も...85

APPENDIX B:
SENTENCE STRUCTURES 87

APPENDIX C:
DICTIONARY 93

PREFACE

Japan-Ease Grammar
makes learning Japanese grammar easy!

Japan-Ease Grammar comprehensively addresses Japanese grammar and emphasizes verb, adjective and copula conjugations. Unlike other Japanese grammar texts, this instructional guide provides an alternative learning method to less efficient standard methods. With its unique learning method, *Japan-Ease Grammar* is an effective independent language learning system. In addition, because *Japan-Ease Grammar* fills textbook learning gaps, it functions as a superb textbook companion in high school and university courses.

Although this book comprehensively addresses Japanese grammar, the prerequisite Japanese knowledge for this book is minimal. The only prerequisite is the ability to read hiragana and katakana characters. To accommodate a reader's limited vocabulary, a dictionary appendix and footnotes are included, listing the words used in example sentences.

Despite minimal prerequisites, this learning system encompasses basic, intermediate, and advanced grammar. For example, it addresses verb grammar from basic conjugations such as the "presumptive" forms to advanced conjugations such as the "passive," "causative," and "causative passive" forms.

Basic through advanced grammar is included in *Japan-Ease Grammar's* verb and adjective conjugation formulas. Learning these formulas instead of tediously memorizing the conjugations of individual verbs and adjectives saves time. To illustrate, instead of memorizing individual verb conjugations, readers learn how to obtain a series of bases for each verb type, and then learn base-containing conjugation formulas that hold true for all verb types.

Both verb conjugation formula charts, adjective conjugation formula charts, and copula charts are provided. The charts allow readers to visualize grammar patterns. The charts also enable readers to quickly look up relevant information.

How else does *Japan-Ease Grammar* simplify the conjugations of verbs, adjectives, and copulas? This book clarifies what standard language learning methods merely imply. For example, traditionally students have been expected to infer through examples that some verbs, when passive, conjugate as a different verb type. In contrast, Pierson explains when and why a verb is conjugated as a different verb type, while also providing detailed examples.

Japan-Ease Grammar also simplifies the conjugations of verbs, adjectives, and copulas by clarifying when and how exceptions occur. For example, standard learning methods do not clearly explain how to conjugate the exceptional verb *aru*. *Japan-Ease Grammar* provides concrete rules regarding how to conjugate *aru*.

Readers learn how to conjugate verbs, adjectives, and copulas within the context of sentences. Example sentences are provided in the verb, adjective, and copula chapters. To provide further context, a relative clause chapter, particle appendix, and sentence structure appendix are also included.

While providing context to verb, adjective, and copula conjugations in the particle section, this book does not explain Japanese grammar in terms of English grammar when doing so would confuse the learner. For example, what is considered an indirect object in Japanese is not always considered an indirect object in English, and the author clearly explains the differences.

So how was this unique learning method in *Japan-Ease Grammar* developed? Tiffany Pierson leveraged her experience as a Japan-America Friendship Scholar, and her Bachelor of Arts from The George Washington University, where she studied Japanese. Furthermore, the author undertook an extensive period of self-directed research. Pierson meticulously analyzed Japanese grammar patterns, penned hundreds of grammatical questions that she addressed to native Japanese speakers, and analyzed the native speakers' answers. The amazing result is the unique and easy learning method found in *Japan-Ease Grammar!*

INTRODUCTION TO DIFFERENCES BETWEEN JAPANESE AND ENGLISH

Unlike English, Japanese does not possess a plural. For this reason, a Japanese noun may be translated as a singular noun in some example sentences in this book, yet may be translated as a plural noun in other example sentences. To illustrate, the noun ほん may be translated as the singular noun "book" in some examples, yet may be translated as the plural noun "books" in other examples.

Another difference between Japanese and English is that Japanese sentences do not contain spaces between words. For this reason, it can be difficult for students of Japanese to identify individual words in sentences. To aid *Japan-Ease Grammar* readers, an interpunct, which is a dot punctuation mark, is inserted between words and particles in example sentences. (For information regarding particles, see the particle appendix.) For example, interpuncts are inserted between わたし (I), particle は, すし (sushi), particle が, and すきだ (like) in the sentence わたし・は・すし・が・すきだ (I like sushi).

Yet another difference between Japanese and English is that Japanese possesses a tense that is unlike any tense in English. This tense is the non-past tense. It is called "non-past tense" instead of "present tense" or "future tense" because a word in non-past tense can be translated as present tense or future tense. For example, an adjective in non-past tense can mean "is the adjective" (the present tense translation) or "will be the adjective" (the future tense translation). To demonstrate, the non-past tense of the adjective "loud" can be translated as "is loud" or "will be loud." As another example of how a word in non-past tense can be translated as present tense or future tense, a verb in non-past tense can mean "does the verb" (the present tense translation) or "will do the verb" (the future tense translation). For instance, the non-past tense of the verb "to fly" can be translated as "flies" or "will fly."

Context indicates whether a verb, adjective, or copula in non-past tense is translated as present tense or future tense. To specify without context that a non-past verb is in present tense instead of future tense, one may employ the progressive form of a verb. The progressive form of a verb means "doing the verb." For instance, the progressive form of the verb "to fly" is "flying." Information about how to obtain the progressive form of a verb is provided in the verb auxiliary section.

Unlike English, Japanese possesses distinct formality levels. *Japan-Ease Grammar* explains both how to conjugate words to create informal sentences and how to conjugate words to create formal sentences. Formal sentences are used between strangers and during professional communication. Professional communication includes workplace communication and teacher-student communication. Informal sentences are used during verbal communication with friends and family. Although verbal communication with friends and family employs informal sentences, formal sentences are written in letters, even in letters to friends and family.

ADJECTIVES

There are two types of adjectives in Japanese, い-adjectives and な-adjectives.

い-Adjectives

Dictionary Form versus Stem

い-adjectives end in い in dictionary form. For example, あかるい is the dictionary form of the い-adjective あかるい (bright).

In contrast, the stem of an い-adjective lacks the final い of dictionary form. For example, the stem of あかるい is あかる.

Conjugation Formula Charts

		Informal			
		Non-Past		Past	
		Affirmative	Negative	Affirmative	Negative
Basic	Dict.		Stem + くない	Stem + かった	Stem + くなかった
Presumptive	Dict. + だろう		Stem + くないだろう	Stem + かった(だ)ろう*	Stem + くなかった(だ)ろう*
Obligation	Stem + くなければなら ない		Stem + くてはならない	NA	NA
ば Conditional	Stem + ければ		Stem + くなければ	Stem + ければ	Stem + くなければ
たら Conditional	Stem + かったら		Stem + くなかったら	Stem + かったら	Stem + くなかったら
Colloquial Conditional	Stem + けりゃ		Stem + くなきゃ	Stem + けりゃ	Stem + くなきゃ
Standard Continuative	Stem + く(て)*		Stem + くな(て)*	Stem + く(て)*	Stem + くな(て)*
たり Continuative	Stem + かったり		Stem + くなかったり	Stem + かったり	Stem + くなかったり

2 • Japan-Ease Grammar

	Non-Past		Formal	
	Affirmative	**Negative**	**Affirmative**	**Negative**
			Past	
			Affirmative	**Negative**
Basic	Dict. + です	Stem + くないです	Stem + かったです	Stem + くなかったです
Presumptive	Dict. + でしょう	Stem + くないでしょう	Stem + かったでしょう	Stem + くなかったでしょう
Obligation	Stem + くなければなりません	Stem + くてはなりません	NA	NA
ば Conditional	Stem + ければ	Stem + くなければ	Stem + ければ	Stem + くなければ
たら Conditional	Stem + かったら	Stem + くなかったら	Stem + かったら	Stem + くなかったら
Standard Continuative	Stem + く(て)*	Stem + くな く(て)*	Stem + く(て)*	Stem + くな く(て)*
たり Continuative	Stem + かったり	Stem + くなかったり	Stem + かったり	Stem + くなかったり

		Informal			
		Non-Past		Past	
		Affirmative	Negative	Affirmative	Negative
Basic		あかるい is bright	あかるくない is not bright	あかるかった was bright	あかるくなかった was not bright
Presumptive		あかるいだろう probably is bright	あかるくないだろう probably is not bright	あかるかった(だ)ろう probably was bright	あかるくなかった(だ)ろう* probably was not bright
Obligation		あかるくなければならない must be bright	あかるくてはならない must not be bright	NA	NA
ば Conditional		あかるければ if is bright	あかるくなければ if is not bright	あかるければ if was bright	あかるくなければ if was not bright
たら Conditional		あかるかったら if is bright	あかるくなかったら if is not bright	あかるかったら if was bright	あかるくなかったら if was not bright
Colloquial Conditional		あかるけりゃ if is bright	あかるくなきゃ if is not bright	あかるけりゃ if was bright	あかるくなきゃ if was not bright
Standard Continuative		あかるく(て)* is bright and	あかるくなく(て)* is not bright and	あかるく(て)* was bright and	あかるくなく(て)* was not bright and
たり Continuative		あかるかったり is bright and	あかるくなかったり is not bright and	あかるかったり was bright and	あかるくなかったり was not bright and

4 • Japan-Ease Grammar

	Formal			
	Non-Past		Past	
	Affirmative	Negative	Affirmative	Negative
Basic	あかるいです is bright	あかるくないです is not bright	あかるかったです was bright	あかるくなかったです was not bright
Presumptive	あかるいでしょう probably is bright	あかるくないでしょう probably is not bright	あかるかったでしょう probably was bright	あかるくなかったでしょう probably was not bright
Obligation	あかるくなければなりません must be bright	あかるくてはなりません must not be bright	NA	NA
ば Conditional	あかるければ if is bright	あかるくなければ if is not bright	あかるければ if was bright	あかるくなければ if was not bright
たら Conditional	あかるかったら if is bright	あかるくなかったら if is not bright	あかるかったら if was bright	あかるくなかったら if was not bright
Standard Continuative	あかるく(て)* is bright and	あかるくな(く)(て)* is not bright and	あかるく(て)* was bright and	あかるくな(く)(て)* was not bright and
たり Continuative	あかるかったり is bright and	あかるくなかったり is not bright and	あかるかったり was bright and	あかるくなかったり was not bright and

*The hiragana in parentheses are normally included; the hiragana in parentheses are omitted. For example, the hiragana だ in the informal presumptive past affirmative formula stem + かった(だ)ろう is normally included. The い-adjective あかるい (bright) conjugated according to the formula stem + かった(だ)ろう is あかるかった(だ)ろう (probably was bright). Thus, あかるかっただろう, which does include だ, is more common than あかるかったろう, which does not include だ.

Adjectives • 5

Exceptional い-Adjective いい

いい (good) is an exceptional い-adjective. Because いい originates from よい, the dictionary form is いい, and the stem is よ. Accordingly, いい is employed when a formula calls for the dictionary form of an い-adjective, whereas よ is employed when a formula calls for the stem of an い-adjective. To demonstrate, いい conjugated according to the informal presumptive non-past affirmative formula dict. + だろう that contains dictionary form is いいだろう (probably is good). In contrast, いい conjugated according to the formula stem + くないだろう that is built on the stem is よくないだろう (probably is not good).

Example Sentence Charts

		Informal	
Form	Placement	Example Sentence	
Basic	Sentence End	ブーケ・は・うつくしい。[1] The bouquet is beautiful.	
Presumptive	Sentence End	チケット・は・たかいだろう。[2] The tickets are probably expensive.	
Obligation	Sentence End	おすもうさん・は・ふとくなければならない。[3] Sumo wrestlers must be fat.	
ば Conditional	Mid-Sentence	はこ・は・おおきければ、おもい。[4] If the boxes are large, they will be heavy.	
たら Conditional	Mid-Sentence	しゅくだい・が・すくなかったら、わたし・は・うれしい。[5] If there is little homework, I am glad.	
Colloquial Conditional	Mid-Sentence	あなた・の・セーター・が・あつけりゃ、あなた・は・さむくない。[6] If your sweater were thick, you wouldn't be cold.	

---

1 ブーケ bouquet • うつくしい beautiful
2 チケット ticket • たかい expensive
3 おすもうさん sumo wrestler • ふとい fat
4 はこ box • おおきい large • おもい heavy
5 しゅくだい homework • すくない scarce; a little • わたし I • うれしい glad
6 あなた you • セーター sweater • あつい thick • さむい cold

Informal		
Form	Placement	Example Sentence
Standard Continuative	Mid-Sentence	その・し・は・ぶっか・が・たかくなくて、はんざい・りつ・が・ひくい。[7] As for that city, the cost of living is not high and the crime rate is low.
たり Continuative	Mid-Sentence	その・えいが・は・こわかったり、おかしかったり・する。*[8] That movie is sometimes scary and sometimes funny.

Formal		
Form	Placement	Example Sentence
Basic	Sentence End	きっさてん・は・ちかいです。[9] A coffee shop is close.
Presumptive	Sentence End	しけん・は・むずかしいでしょう。[10] The test will probably be difficult.
Obligation	Sentence End	がっこう・で・スカート・の・たけ・は・ながくなければなりません。[11] The length of a skirt must be long at school.
ば Conditional	Mid-Sentence	クラス・が・はやければ、わたし・は・じゅぎょうちゅう・に・ねむいです。[12] If the class is early, I will be sleepy in class.
たら Conditional	Mid-Sentence	プロダクトデザイン・が・わるかったら、プロダクト・の・じゅよう・は・すくないです。[13] If the product design is poor, demand for the product will be small.

---

7   その that • し city • ぶっか cost of living • たかい high; expensive • はんざい crime • りつ rate • ひくい low
8   その that • えいが movie • こわい scary • おかしい funny • する to do
9   きっさてん coffee shop • ちかい close
10 しけん test • むずかしい difficult
11 がっこう school • スカート skirt • たけ length • ながい long
12 クラス class • はやい early • わたし I • じゅぎょうちゅう while in class • ねむい sleepy
13 プロダクトデザイン product design • わるい bad • プロダクト product • じゅよう demand • すくない a little

Formal		
Form	Placement	Example Sentence
Standard Continuative	Mid-Sentence	その・やきゅう・の・カード・は・すくなくて、たかいです。[14] That baseball card is rare and expensive.
たり Continuative	Mid-Sentence	その・みせ・の・かかく・は・やすかったり、たかかったり・します。*[15] That store's prices are sometimes cheap and sometimes expensive.

*The continuative form explanation that follows later explains why the sentences containing たり continuative い-adjectives contain a conjugation of the verb する (to do) such as します.

Conditional い-Adjectives

The non-past affirmative and past affirmative formulas in the respective conditional rows are the same. For example, both the formal ば conditional non-past affirmative formula and formal ば conditional past affirmative formula are stem + ければ.

In the same way as the non-past affirmative and past affirmative formulas are the same, the non-past negative and past negative formulas in the respective conditional rows are the same. For example, both the informal colloquial conditional non-past negative formula and informal colloquial conditional past negative formula are stem + くなきゃ.

Because the non-past affirmative and past affirmative formulas are the same, and the non-past negative and past negative formulas are the same, context indicates whether a ば conditional, たら conditional, or colloquial conditional い-adjective is in non-past or past tense. For example, context indicates that the ば conditional い-adjective よければ is in non-past tense in the sentence てんき・が・よければ、イベント・に・ひと・が・おおいだろう (if the weather is good, there probably will be a lot of people at the event). This context is derived from the clause イベント・に・ひと・が・おおいだろう. The clause イベント・に・ひと・が・おおいだろう is in non-past tense because おお

---

14 その that • やきゅう baseball • カード card • すくない scarce • たかい expensive
15 その that • みせ store • かかく price • やすい cheap • たかい expensive • する to do

いだろう (probably will be many) is the い-adjective おおい (many) conjugated according to the non-past formula dict. + だろう. Since the clause イベント・に・ひと・が・おおいだろう is in non-past tense, よければ is in non-past tense. As a non-past tense い-adjective, よければ means "if it is good" instead of "if it was good."[16]

Although よければ is in non-past tense in the sentence てんき・が・よければ、イベント・に・ひと・が・おおいだろう, context indicates that よければ is in past tense in the sentence てんき・が・よければ、イベント・に・ひと・が・おおかっただろう (if the weather had been good, there probably would have been a lot of people at the event). This context results from the clause イベント・に・ひと・が・おおかっただろう. The clause イベント・に・ひと・が・おおかっただろう is in past tense because おおかっただろう (probably would have been many) is the い-adjective おおい (many) conjugated according to the past formula stem + かっただろう. As the clause イベント・に・ひと・が・おおかっただろう is in past tense, よければ is in past tense. In other words, よければ means "if it had been good" instead of "if it is good."

Although a ば conditional, たら conditional, or colloquial conditional い-adjective can create a conditional past tense phrase, an い-adjective can also form a conditional past tense phrase by modifying the noun ばあい (meaning "case"), thereby creating a relative clause. As explained in the relative clause section of this book, informal basic い-adjectives can modify nouns. Since ひくかった is the い-adjective ひくい (low) conjugated according to the informal basic formula stem + かった, ひくかった can modify the noun ばあい. The relative clause ひくかった・ばあい literally translates as "case that it had been low" but means "if it had been low."

A relative clause that contains a modifying い-adjective and the modified noun ばあい ends a mid-sentence clause, instead of a sentence, like ば conditional, たら conditional, and colloquial conditional い-adjectives do. For example, the relative clause かかく・が・ひくかった・ばあい (if the price had been low), which contains the modifying い-adjective ひくかった and the modified noun ばあい, ends the mid-sentence clause in the sentence かかく・が・ひくかった・ばあい、はんばい・りょう・は・おおかったでしょう. The sentence かかく・が・ひくかった・ばあい、はんばい・りょう・は・おおかったでしょう

---

16   てんき weather • いい good • イベント event • ひと person • おおい many

literally translates to "as for the case that the price had been low, the number of sales probably would have been many," but means "if the price had been low, there probably would have been many sales."[17]

Continuative い-Adjectives

Standard continuative い-adjectives mean "is/is not/was/was not the い-adjective and." For example, in the sentence スープ・は・あつくて、あまくて、からかったです (the soup was hot and sweet and spicy), あつくて, which is the い-adjective あつい (hot) conjugated according to the standard continuative affirmative formula stem + く(て), means "was hot and." Likewise, あまくて, which is the い-adjective あまい (sweet) conjugated according to the standard continuative affirmative formula stem + く(て), means "was sweet and."[18]

Unlike standard continuative い-adjectives, たり continuative い-adjectives can mean "in some instances is/is not/was/was not the い-adjective." For example, in the sentence ゆうめいじん・は・せ・が・たかかったり、せ・が・ひくかったり・する, たかかったり, which is the い-adjective たかい (tall) conjugated according to the たり continuative affirmative formula stem + かったり, means "in some instances is tall." Likewise, ひくかったり, which is the い-adjective ひくい (short) conjugated according to the たり continuative affirmative formula stem + かったり, means "in some instances is short." Given these points, the sentence means "celebrities are in some instances tall and in some instances short." In other words, the sentence means "some celebrities are tall and some are short."[19]

All い-adjectives creating a たり continuative list should be in たり continuative form. For example, in the sentence ゆうめいじん・は・せ・が・たかかったり、せ・が・ひくかったり・する, the い-adjectives たかかったり and ひくかったり are in たり continuative form.

17　かかく price • ひくい low • ばあい case • はんばい sales • りょう amount • おおい many

18　スープ soup • あつい hot • あまい sweet • からい spicy

19　ゆうめいじん celebrity • せ height • たかい tall • ひくい low • する to do

Although all い-adjectives creating a たり continuative list should be in たり continuative form, a たり continuative い-adjective cannot end a sentence. As the example sentence charts indicate, たり continuative い-adjectives are placed mid-sentence rather than at the end of sentences. Since a たり continuative い-adjective cannot end a sentence, the verb する (to do) ends the sentence ゆうめいじん・は・せ・が・たかかったり、せ・が・ひくかったり・する.

Obligation い-Adjectives

The informal obligation non-past affirmative formula is stem + くなければならない. This formula stem + くなければならない is a combination of the ば conditional negative formula stem + くなければ (meaning "if not the い-adjective") and ならない. ならない (will not become) is the informal basic non-past negative form of the verb なる (to become). As a result, stem + くなければならない literally translates as "if not the い-adjective, will not become." For example, はやくなければならない, which is the い-adjective はやい (early) conjugated according to the formula stem + くなければならない, literally translates as "if not early, will not become."

Although the literal translation of stem + くなければならない is "if not the い-adjective, will not become," the meaning of stem + くなければならない is "must be the い-adjective." For example, はやくなければならない, which is the い-adjective はやい conjugated according to the formula stem + くなければならない, means "must be early."

Whereas the *informal* obligation non-past affirmative formula is stem + くなければならない (must be the い-adjective), the *formal* obligation non-past affirmative formula is stem + くなければなりません (must be the い-adjective). The informal formula stem + くなければならない contains ならない (will not become), which is the *informal* basic non-past negative form of the verb なる (to become), and the formal formula stem + くなければなりません contains なりません (will not become), which is the *formal* basic non-past negative form of the verb なる.

な-Adjectives

Dictionary Form versus Stem

A な-adjective ends in な in dictionary form. For example, げんきな is the dictionary form of the な-adjective げんきな (well).

In contrast, the stem of a な-adjective lacks the final な of dictionary form. For example, the stem of げんきな is げんき.

な-Adjective Conjugation Formulas

No な-adjective conjugation formula charts are provided. This is because the formulas for obtaining basic, presumptive, obligation, ば conditional, たら conditional, なら conditional, colloquial conditional, standard continuative, and たり continuative な-adjectives are simply stem + a copula in the relevant cell of the copula charts. (The copula charts are located in the copula chapter.) For instance, the な-adjective informal presumptive past affirmative formula is stem + だった(だ)ろう because the informal presumptive past affirmative copula is だった(だ)ろう. To illustrate, the な-adjective しょうじきな (honest) conjugated according to the formula stem + だった(だ)ろう is しょうじきだった(だ)ろう (probably was honest).

Adjectives, Hiragana, and Katakana

Whereas hiragana spells native words, katakana spells foreign words and emphasized words. Foreign words derive from languages such as English, French, German, Portuguese, and Dutch. Emphasized words include onomatopoeias (such as ワンワン, meaning "woof"), Japanese company names (such as パナソニック, meaning "Panasonic"), scientific words (such as ガン, meaning "cancer"), and native words normally spelled with hiragana but spelled with katakana for emphasis, such as on advertisements.

As hiragana and katakana spell different types of words, some adjectives are spelled with hiragana and some adjectives are spelled with katakana. Hiragana is used for い-adjectives. This is because い-adjectives are native adjectives and hiragana spells native words. For example, うすい (thin), being an い-adjective, is written with hiragana.

Like い-adjectives, native な-adjectives are written with hiragana. Native な-adjectives are written with hiragana because hiragana spells native words. For example, as a native な-adjective, すきな (like) is written with hiragana.

Although native な-adjectives do not contain katakana, foreign な-adjectives do. Specifically, foreign な-adjectives contain a katakana stem (the portion of the な-adjective preceding the final な of dictionary form). Foreign な-adjectives contain a katakana stem because katakana spells foreign words. In addition to a katakana stem, foreign な-adjectives contain a hiragana な for conjugation. Although the stem of a な-adjective remains unchanged during conjugation, the hiragana な is replaced with a hiragana copula. (See the prior section "な-adjective conjugation formulas" for information regarding な-adjective conjugations.) An example of a foreign な-adjective is ハンサムな (handsome), which comprises a katakana stem and hiragana な.

Noun Form

Both い-adjectives and な-adjectives can become nouns as per the formula stem + さ. For example, the い-adjective つよい (strong) conjugated according to the formula stem + さ is つよさ (strength). Likewise, the な-adjective ていねいな (polite) conjugated according to the formula stem + さ is ていねいさ (politeness).

ADVERBS

Formula Chart

な-adjectives and い-adjectives can become adverbs as per the formulas below.

	Formula	Example Adjective	Example Adverb
い-Adjectives	Stem + く	うれしい happy	うれしく happily
な-Adjectives	Stem + に	じょうずな skillful	じょうずに skillfully

Adverb Endings

Though な-adjectives can become adverbs ending in に as per the formula stem + に, and い-adjectives can become adverbs ending in く as per the formula stem + く, not all adverbs end in く or に. Not all adverbs end in く or に because not all adverbs derive from adjectives. For example, the adverbs たくさん (many) and ゆっくり (slowly), which do not end in く or に, do not derive from adjectives.

Adverb Placement

An adverb must be positioned in a sentence so that the adverb assigns meaning to the intended verb. However, an adverb's placement in a sentence is otherwise flexible. For example, consider the placement of the adverb はやく (quickly) in the sentence わたし・が・がっこう・に・はやく・いく (I go to school quickly). The sentence can also be written as わたし・が・はやく・がっこう・に・いく, with はやく before がっこう (school). The meaning of the sentence is unchanged.[20]

---

20   わたし I • がっこう school • はやい quick • いく to go

COPULAS

Copulas and Nouns

Copulas express nouns in basic, presumptive, obligation, ば conditional, たら conditional, なら conditional, colloquial conditional, standard continuative, and たり continuative forms by immediately following nouns. For example, the informal presumptive non-past affirmative copula だろう (is probably) expresses a noun in informal presumptive non-past affirmative form. だろう follows the noun えいが (movie) of the phrase いい・えいが (good movie) to form いい・えいがだろう (is probably a good movie). As another example, the informal presumptive non-past negative copula で(は)ないだろう (is probably not) expresses a noun in informal presumptive non-past negative form. で(は)ないだろう follows the noun えいが (movie) of the phrase いい・えいが (good movie) to form いい・えいがで(は)ないだろう (is probably not a good movie).[21]

Copulas and な-Adjectives

In addition to expressing nouns in various forms, copulas express な-adjectives in basic, presumptive, obligation, ば conditional, たら conditional, なら conditional, colloquial conditional, standard continuative, and たり continuative forms. The formulas for conjugating な-adjectives into the said forms are

---

21   いい good • えいが movie

stem + a copula in the corresponding cell of the copula charts. For example, the な-adjective formal たら conditional non-past affirmative formulas are stem + だったら and stem + でしたら because the formal たら conditional non-past affirmative copulas are だったら and でしたら. To demonstrate, the formal たら conditional non-past affirmative forms of the な-adjective がんこな (stubborn) are がんこだったら (if is stubborn) and がんこでしたら (if is stubborn) as the stem of がんこな is がんこ.

Emphasizing は

は (pronounced in this instance as "wa" although the hiragana は is normally pronounced as "ha") may be inserted after the initial で of negative copulas that begin with で. For example, は may be inserted after で in the informal basic non-past negative copula でない to obtain ではない.

The は that may be inserted after the initial で of negative copulas that begin with で emphasizes that a copula is negative. For example, the phrase こちょうでない, which includes the noun こちょう meaning "exaggeration" and the copula でない that does not contain は, translates as "not an exaggeration," while こちょうではない, which does contain は, translates as "*not* an exaggeration."

Although は emphasizes that a copula is negative, は does not alter a copula's formality level. For example, the informal basic non-past negative copula でない (is not), which does not contain は, and the informal basic non-past negative copula ではない (is not), which does contain は, are equally informal. Likewise, the formal basic non-past negative copula でないです (is not), which does not contain は, and the formal basic non-past negative copula ではないです (is not), which does contain は, are equally formal.

Beginnings では and じゃ

The initial では of negative copulas that begin with では may be replaced with じゃ because じゃ is a contraction of では. For example, the では of the informal basic non-past negative copula ではない (is not) may be replaced with じゃ to form the informal basic non-past negative copula じゃない (is not).

Replacing では with じゃ makes a copula slightly less formal. For example, although the informal basic non-past negative copula ではない (is not) and the informal basic non-past negative copula じゃない (is not) are both informal, じゃない is slightly more informal than でない. Likewise, although the formal basic non-past negative copula ではないです (is not) and the formal basic non-past negative copula じゃないです (is not) are both formal, ではないです is slightly more formal than じゃないです.

Colloquial Conditional Copulas

A speaker selects a colloquial conditional copula instead of a ば conditional, たら conditional, or なら conditional copula to emphasize informality. A speaker emphasizing informality will also replace the では beginning of a negative copula with じゃ because doing so makes a copula slightly more informal. Accordingly, the colloquial conditional negative copula じゃなきゃ, which contains the beginning じゃ, is almost always used instead of the colloquial conditional negative copula ではなきゃ, which contains the beginning では. To demonstrate, the sentence あめじゃなきゃ、かさ・が・ひつようじゃない (if it is not rainy, an umbrella is not necessary), which contains じゃなきゃ, would more likely be stated than the sentence あめではなきゃ、かさ・が・ひつようじゃない (if it is not rainy, an umbrella is not necessary), which contains ではなきゃ.[22]

Copula Charts

In a chart cell that contains two copulas, the most common copula is listed first in the chart cell and the least common copula is listed last in the chart cell. For example, でした is the more common formal basic past affirmative copula so it is listed first in the formal basic past affirmative chart cell. Conversely, だったです is the less common formal basic past affirmative copula so it is listed last in the formal basic past affirmative chart cell.

22　あめ rain • かさ umbrella • ひつような necessary

	Informal			
	Non-Past		Past	
	Affirmative	Negative	Affirmative	Negative
Basic	だ; である is	ではない is not	だった; であった was	ではなかった was not
Presumptive	だろう probably is	ではないだろう probably is not	だった(だ)ろう* probably was	ではなかった(だ)ろう* probably was not
Obligation	でなければならない must be	であってはならない must not be	NA	NA
ば Conditional	であれば if is	でなければ if is not	であれば if was	でなければ if was not
たら Conditional	だったら if is	ではなかったら if is not	だったら if was	ではなかったら if was not
なら Conditional	なら(ば)** if is	NA	なら(ば)** if was	NA
Colloquial Conditional	でありや if is	でなきや if is not	でありや if was	でなきや if was not
Standard Continuative	で is and	でなく(て)* is not and	で was and	でなく(て)* was not and
たり Continuative	だったり is and	ではなかったり is not and	だったり was and	ではなかったり was not and

	Formal					
	Non-Past		Past			
	Affirmative	Negative	Affirmative	Negative		
Basic	です is	ではないです is not	でした; だったです was	ではなかったです was not		
Presumptive	でしょう probably is	ではないでしょう probably is not	だったでしょう probably was	ではなかったでしょう probably was not		
Obligation	でなければなりません must be	であってはなりません must not be	NA	NA		
ば Conditional	であれば if is	でなければ if is not	であれば if was	でなければ if was not		
たら Conditional	だったら; でしたら if is	でなかったら if is not	だったら; でしたら if was	でなかったら if was not		
なら Conditional	なら(ば)** if is	NA	なら(ば)** if was	NA		
Standard Continuative	でして** is and	でなく(て)* is not and	でして** was and	でなく(て)* was not and		
たり Continuative	だったり; でしたり is and	でなかったり is not and	だったり; でしたり was and	でなかったり was not and		

*The hiragana in parentheses are normally included; the copulas are colloquial when the hiragana in parentheses are omitted. For example, the hiragana て in the informal standard continuative non-past negative copula でなく(て) (is not and) is normally included. That being the case, でなくて, which does include て, is more common than でなく, which does not include て.

**The hiragana in parentheses are normally not included. For example, the hiragana ば in the formal なら conditional non-past affirmative copula なら(ば) (if is) is normally not included. Thus, なら, which does not include ば, is more common than ならば, which does include ば.

Copulas • 21

Example Sentence Charts

Informal		
Form	Placement	Example Sentence
Basic	Sentence End	プレゼントだ。[23] It is a present.
Presumptive	Sentence End	じょうだんだっただろう。[24] It probably was a joke.
Obligation	Sentence End	プレジデント・は・うまい・はなしてでなければならない。*[25] The president must be a skillful speaker.
ば Conditional	Mid-Sentence	しんきろうであれば、みずではない。[26] If it is a mirage, then it is not water.
たら Conditional	Mid-Sentence	バンド・は・にんきだったら、チケット・は・かんばいだろう。[27] If the band is popular, the tickets will probably sell out.
なら Conditional	Mid-Sentence	あなた・が・まちがい・なら、わたし・も・まちがいだ。[28] If you are wrong, then I'm also wrong.
Colloquial Conditional	Mid-Sentence	ホラーえいがでありゃ、わたし・は・すきじゃない。[29] If it is a horror movie, then I will not like it.
Standard Continuative	Mid-Sentence	ゆか・は・ドライでなくて、つるつるです。[30] The floor is not dry and is slippery.
たり Continuative	Mid-Sentence	りんじん・は・しずかだったり、うるさかったり・する。**[31] The neighbors are sometimes quiet and sometimes loud.

---

23 プレゼント present
24 じょうだん joke
25 プレジデント president • うまい skillful • はなして speaker
26 しんきろう mirage • みず water
27 バンド band • にんきな popular • チケット ticket • かんばい sold out
28 あなた you • まちがい error • わたし I
29 ホラーえいが horror movie • わたし I • すきな like
30 ゆか floor • ドライな dry • つるつる slippery
31 りんじん neighbor • しずかな quiet • うるさい loud • する to do
32 たいへんな great • めいよ honor

Formal		
Form	Placement	Example Sentence
Basic	Sentence End	たいへんな・めいよです。*32 It is a great honor.
Presumptive	Sentence End	ほんとうでしょう。33 It is probably true.
Obligation	Sentence End	しょうにん・は・しょうじきでなければなりません。34 The witness must be honest.
ば Conditional	Mid-Sentence	アイテム・は・１００(ひゃく)・ねん・ものであれば、たしか に・アンティークです。35 If the item is 100 years old (a 100 years thing), then it is certainly an antique.
たら Conditional	Mid-Sentence	せいひん・が・にんきだったら、かいしゃ・は・せいこうでし ょう。36 If the product is popular, the company will probably be a success.
なら Conditional	Mid-Sentence	かのじょ・は・べんごしなら、あまり・ひま・が・ないでしょう。37 If she is a lawyer, she probably doesn't have much free time.
Standard Continuative	Mid-Sentence	いえ・は・しずかで、くらいです。38 The house is silent and dark.
たり Continuative	Mid-Sentence	わたし・の・はだ・は・オイリーだったり、かんそうだったり・ します。**39 My skin is sometimes oily and sometimes dry.

*As explained in the relative clause chapter, the dictionary form of an い-adjective can modify a noun to create a relative clause that means "noun that is the い-adjective." For example, the dictionary form of the い-adjective うまい (skillful) modifies the noun はなして (speaker) in the relative clause うまい・はなして (speaker that is skillful; skillful speaker).

In the same way as the dictionary form of an い-adjective can modify a noun to create a relative clause meaning "noun that is the い-adjective," the dictionary form of a な-adjective can modify a noun to create a relative clause meaning "noun that is the な-adjective." For example, the dictionary form of the な-adjective たいへんな (great) modifies the noun めいよ (honor) in the relative clause たいへんな・めいよ (honor that is great; great honor).

**The continuative form explanation that follows details why the sentences containing たり continuative copulas possess a conjugation of the verb する (to do) such as します.

---

33 ほんとうな true
34 しょうにん witness • しょうじきな honest
35 アイテム item • ひゃく 100 • ねん year • もの thing • たしかに certainly • アンティーク antique
36 せいひん product • にんきな popular • かいしゃ company • せいこう success
37 かのじょ she • べんごし lawyer • あまり not much • ひま free time • ない nonexistent
38 いえ house • しずかな quiet • くらい dark
39 わたし I • はだ skin • オイリーな oily • かんそう dry • する to do

Conditional Copulas

The non-past affirmative chart cell and past affirmative chart cell contain the same copulas in the respective conditional rows. For example, both the non-past affirmative cell and the past affirmative cell in the informal たら conditional row contain the copula だったら. Likewise, both the non-past affirmative chart cell and the past affirmative chart cell in the formal たら conditional row contain the copulas だったら and でしたら.

Similar to how the non-past affirmative cell and past affirmative cell contain the same copulas in the respective conditional rows, the non-past negative cell and past negative cell contain the same copulas in the respective conditional rows. For example, both the non-past negative and the past negative cells in the informal colloquial conditional row contain the copula でなきゃ. As another example, both the non-past negative cell and the past negative cell in the formal ば conditional row contain the copula でなければ.

Because the non-past affirmative and past affirmative cells contain the same copulas, and the non-past negative and the past negative cells contain the same copulas, in the respective conditional rows, context indicates whether a conditional copula is in non-past tense or past tense. For example, context indicates that the ば conditional copula であれば is in non-past tense in the sentence あなた・が・ひまであれば、いい (if you are free, that's great). This context results from the clause いい. Because the い-adjective いい employs the non-past formula dict., the clause いい is in non-past tense. Since the clause いい is in non-past tense, であれば is in non-past tense. As a non-past tense copula, であれば means "if are" instead of "if were."[40]

While であれば is in non-past tense in the sentence あなた・が・ひまであれば、いい, context indicates that であれば is in past tense in the sentence あなた・が・ひまであれば、よかった (if you had been free, that would have been great; I wish you would have been free). This context results from the clause よかった. The clause よかった is formed from the stem of the い-adjective いい (good), which is よ, conjugated according to the past formula stem + かった. Since the clause よかった is in past tense, であれば is in past tense. As a past tense copula, であれば means "if had been" instead of "if are."

40　あなた you • ひまな free • いい good

Although a ば conditional, たら conditional, なら conditional, or colloquial conditional copula can follow a noun, or な-adjective stem, to create a conditional past tense phrase, a noun or な-adjective can also form a conditional past tense phrase by modifying the noun ばあい (meaning "case"), thereby creating a relative clause. The relative clause section of this book explains how nouns and な-adjectives modify nouns. For instance, the relative clause section explains that a noun + だった can modify a noun to create a relative clause in which the modifying noun is past affirmative. For example, バラだった, which contains the noun バラ and the copula だった, can modify the noun ばあい. The relative clause バラだった・ばあい literally translates as "case that they were roses" but means "if they were roses."

A relative clause that contains either a modifying noun or modifying な-adjective, and contains the modified noun ばあい, ends a mid-sentence clause, instead of a sentence, as do ば conditional, たら conditional, なら conditional and colloquial conditional copulas. For example, the relative clause バラだった・ばあい (if they were roses), which contains the modifying noun バラ and the modified noun ばあい, ends the mid-sentence clause in the sentence はな・が・バラだったばあい、かれ・は・あなた・が・だいすきだ. This sentence literally translates to "as for the case that the flowers were roses, he likes you very much," but means "if the flower were roses, then he likes you very much."[41]

Continuative Copulas

Standard continuative copulas mean "is/is not/was/was not and." For example, in the sentence てんき・は・くもりで、あつくて、むしあつかったです (the weather was cloudy, hot, and humid), the phrase くもりで, which contains the noun くもり (cloudy weather) and the standard continuative affirmative copula で, means "was cloudy and."[42]

Unlike standard continuative copulas, たり continuative copulas can mean "in some instances is/is not/was/was not." For example, in the

---

41 はな flower • バラ rose • ばあい case • かれ he • あなた you • だいすきな like very much
42 てんき weather • くもり cloudy weather • あつい hot • むしあつい humid

sentence バー・は・にぎやかだったり、にぎやかでなかったり・する, the phrase にぎやかだったり, which contains the stem of the な-adjective にぎやかな (lively) and the たり continuative affirmative copula だったり, means "in some instances is lively." Likewise, the phrase にぎやかでなかったり, which contains the stem of the な-adjective にぎやかな and the たり continuative negative copula でなかったり, means "in some instances is not lively." Given these points, the sentence means "the bar in some instances is lively and in some instances is not lively." In other words, the sentence means "the bar is sometimes lively and sometimes not lively."[43]

All nouns and な-adjectives creating a たり continuative list should be followed with a たり continuative copula. For example, in the sentence バー・は・にぎやかだったり、にぎやかでなかったり・する, the stems of にぎやかな are followed with たり continuative copulas.

Although all nouns and な-adjectives creating a たり continuative list should be in たり continuative form, a たり continuative copula cannot end a sentence. As the example sentence charts indicate, たり continuative copulas are placed mid-sentence rather than at the end of sentences. Because a たり continuative copula cannot end a sentence, the verb する (to do) ends the sentence バー・は・にぎやかだったり、にぎやかでなかったり・する.

Obligation Copulas

The informal obligation non-past affirmative copula is でなければならない (must be). This copula でなければならない is a combination of the ば conditional negative copula でなければ (meaning "if not") and ならない. ならない (will not become) is the informal basic non-past negative form of the verb なる (to become). As a result, でなければならない literally translates as "if not, will not become." For example, きんべんな・じゅうぎょういんでなければならない, which contains the phrase きんべんな・じゅうぎょういん (hardworking employee) and the copula でなければならない, literally translates as "if not a hardworking employee, will not become."[44]

---

43   バー bar • にぎやかな bustling • する to do
44   きんべんな diligent • じゅうぎょういん employee

Although the copula でなければならない literally translates as "if not, will not become," でなければならない means "must be." For example, きんべんな・じゅうぎょういんでなければならない, which contains きんべんな・じゅうぎょういん (hardworking employee) and the copula でなければならない, means "must be a hardworking employee."

Similar to the *informal* obligation non-past affirmative copula でなければならない (must be) is the *formal* obligation non-past affirmative copula でなければなりません (must be). While the informal copula でなければならない contains ならない (will not become), which is the *informal* basic non-past negative form of the verb なる (to become), the formal copula でなければなりません contains なりません (will not become), which is the *formal* basic non-past negative form of the verb なる.

ある-Copulas

Some copulas, which are called "ある-copulas" in this book, contain a conjugation of the verb ある. (The verb ある means "to exist.") Specifically, affirmative ある-copulas are made up of で (the beginning of affirmative ある-copulas) and a conjugation of the verb ある. In a like manner, negative ある-copulas are made up of で, では, or じゃ (the beginnings of negative ある-copulas), and a conjugation of the verb ある. For example, である, which contains で and the dictionary form of ある, is an ある-copula.

The verb ある is an exceptional verb. In some instances, ある is conjugated like a regular verb. However, in other instances ある is replaced with the い-adjective ない (meaning "nonexistent"). Then, ない is conjugated according to the appropriate formula in the い-adjective formula charts. For this reason, some ある-copulas contain a conjugation of the い-adjective ない. For example, でない, which contains で and the dictionary form of ない, is an ある-copula.

For more information regarding how ある is conjugated as an exceptional verb, see the verb chapter of this book. An explanation regarding when ある is replaced with the い-adjective ない, and how ある and ない are conjugated, is provided in the verb chapter.

VERBS

Bases

In this book, "B1," "B2," "B3," "B4," "B5," "Bて," and "Bた" respectively stand for "base one," "base two," "base three," "base four," "base five," "base て," and "base た."

	う-Verbs	る-Verbs
B1	～(あ)/わ*	Stem
B2	～(い)	Stem
B3	～(う)	～る
B4	～(え)	～れ
B5	～(お)う	～よう
Bて	See separate table.	～て
Bた		～た

う-Verb Bて and Bた	
If B3 ends in:	Replace the final hiragana of B3 with:
う, つ, or る	って or った
ぬ, ぶ, or む	んで or んだ
く	いて or いた
ぐ	いで or いだ
す	して or した

	Example Using う-Verb ならう (to learn)	Example Using る-Verb すてる (to dispose)
B1	ならわ	すて
B2	ならい	すて
B3	ならう	すてる
B4	ならえ	すてれ
B5	ならおう	すてよう
Bて	ならって	すてて
Bた	ならった	すてた

う-Verbs

An う-verb ends in the hiragana う, つ, る, ぬ, ぶ, む, く, ぐ or す in B3 (dictionary form).

When changing B3 to B1, B2, B4, or B5, the final hiragana of B3 is replaced with a hiragana of the same row in the hiragana chart. (It is assumed that the hiragana chart is oriented so that rows are listed by consonant and columns are listed by vowel. See the following hiragana chart.) For example, consider how the final hiragana of the B3 まつ (to wait) is replaced with a hiragana of the same row when obtaining B1, B2, B4, or B5. The last hiragana of まつ is つ. つ is of the "t" row of the hiragana chart. The "t" row contains the hiragana た, ち, つ, て, and と. (ち is of the "t" row, but the pronunciation is "chi," which does not contain a "t." Although the pronunciation of a hiragana may be different from the combination of the row consonant and column vowel, all hiragana are considered of their assigned row and column.) Because the "t" row contains the hiragana た, ち, つ, て, and と, the つ of B3 まつ is replaced with た, ち, て, or と depending on whether one is obtaining B1, B2, B4, or B5.

When changing B3 to B1, B2, B4, or B5, the hiragana that replaces the final hiragana of B3 is of the column indicated by the base formula. For example, the parentheses in B2 formula ～(い) indicate that the hiragana that replaces the final hiragana つ of the B3 まつ is of the い column. Among the aforementioned hiragana た, ち, て, and と, the hiragana ち is of the い column. Thus, the つ of B3 まつ is replaced with ち. まち is the B2 of まつ.

When changing B3 to B5, う follows the hiragana that replaces the final hiragana of B3. This is because the B5 formula is ～(お)う. The B5 formula

〜(お)う indicates that the hiragana う follows a hiragana of the お column and of the same row as the final hiragana of B3. To illustrate, consider how to change the B3 あるく (to walk) to B5. The last hiragana of あるく is く. く is of the "k" row of the hiragana chart. The "k" row contains the hiragana か, き, く, け, and こ. Among the aforementioned hiragana か, き, く, け, and こ, the hiragana こ is of the お column. Thus, こ replaces the く of the B3 あるく to obtain あるこ. As the hiragana う follows the hiragana こ, the B5 of "to walk" is あるこう.

There is an exception to the rule that the final hiragana of B3 is replaced with a hiragana of the same row when obtaining B1, B2, B4, or B5. *う-verbs that end in the hiragana う (rather than つ, る, ぬ, ぶ, む, く, ぐ or す) in B3 adopt わ in B1. For example, the B1 of かう (to buy) is かわ.

Hiragana Chart

	A Column	I Column	U Column	E Column	O Column
Vowel-Only Row	あ (a)	い (i)	う (u)	え (e)	お (o)
K Row	か (ka)	き (ki)	く (ku)	け (ke)	こ (ko)
G Row	が (ga)	ぎ (gi)	ぐ (gu)	げ (ge)	ご (go)
S Row	さ (sa)	し (shi)	す (su)	せ (se)	そ (so)
Z Row	ざ (za)	じ (ji)	ず (zu)	ぜ (ze)	ぞ (zo)
T Row	た (ta)	ち (chi)	つ (tsu)	て (te)	と (to)
D Row	だ (da)	ぢ (ji)	づ (zu)	で (de)	ど (do)
N Row	な (na)	に (ni)	ぬ (nu)	ね (ne)	の (no)
H Row	は (ha)	ひ (hi)	ふ (fu)	へ (he)	ほ (ho)
B Row	ば (ba)	び (bi)	ぶ (bu)	べ (be)	ぼ (bo)
P Row	ぱ (pa)	ぴ (pi)	ぷ (pu)	ぺ (pe)	ぽ (po)
M Row	ま (ma)	み (mi)	む (mu)	め (me)	も (mo)
Y Row	や (ya)		ゆ (yu)		よ (yo)
R Row	ら (ra)	り (ri)	る (ru)	れ (re)	ろ (ro)
Misc. Row	わ (wa)				を (o)
Misc. Row	ん (n)				

Exceptional Verb いく

The Bて and Bた of the う-verb いく (to go) are exceptions to the う-verb conjugation rules. According to a preceding table, the final く of an う-verb ending in く in B3 should be replaced with いて to form Bて. The table also states that the final く of an う-verb ending in く in B3 should be replaced with いた to form Bた. One would therefore expect the Bて of いく to be いいて and the Bた of いく to be いいた. However, the Bて of いく is いって and the Bた of いく is いった.

る-Verbs

A る-verb ends in 〜(い)る or 〜(え)る in B3 (dictionary form). In other words, the second to last hiragana ends in an い or え sound (is of the い or え column in the hiragana chart) and the last hiragana is る. For example, しんじる (to believe) and かんがえる (to think) are る-verbs.

When changing B3 to another base, the final る of B3 is either omitted or replaced. For example, because the B2 formula is stem, the る of B3 こたえる (to answer) is omitted to obtain B2. Thus, こたえ is the B2 of こたえる. As another example, because the B4 formula is 〜れ, the る of B3 こたえる is replaced with れ to obtain B4. こたえれ is the B4 of こたえる.

Although some verbs end in 〜(い)る or 〜(え)る, they are う-verbs and conjugate as such. For example, はいる (to enter) is an う-verb even though the B3 ends in 〜(い)る like a る-verb. There is no way to identify by means of the B3 whether a verb ending in 〜(い)る or 〜(え)る in B3 is a る-verb or an う-verb. Accordingly, one must memorize that certain verbs that end in 〜(い)る or 〜(え)る in B3 are actually う-verbs. It is important to do so because knowing the verb type is necessary to correctly conjugate the bases. For example, if one mistakenly thought はいる was a る-verb, one would incorrectly believe the B5 of はいる to be はいよう. As はいる is an う-verb, the B5 of はいる is actually はいろう.

Irregular Verbs

する (to do) and くる (to come) are irregular verbs. When changing a base, the verbs are entirely replaced. For example, the following chart indicates that the B4 of する is すれ, while the Bて of する is して.

	する (to do)	くる (to come)
B1	し	こ
B2	し	き
B3	する	くる
B4	すれ	くれ
B5	しよう	こよう
Bて	して	きて
Bた	した	きた

Some verbs consist of a noun and the irregular verb する (to do) that follows said noun. For example, the verb べんきょうする (to study) contains the noun べんきょう (studying) and the verb する.

To conjugate verbs that consist of a noun and the verb する, simply conjugate する. For example, because the B2 of する is し, べんきょうする conjugated according to the formula B2 + ませんでした (did not do the verb) is べんきょうしませんでした (did not study).

Verb Stems and Kanji

Japanese has three writing systems. These writing systems are hiragana, katakana, and kanji. Whereas hiragana and katakana are writing systems made up of symbols representing syllables, kanji is a writing system made up of symbols simultaneously representing meaning and a phonetic reading. Kanji replace hiragana and katakana in nouns, verbs, adjectives, and adverbs. Since thousands of kanji exist, a reader can easily identify individual words in a sentence with kanji even though Japanese sentences do not contain spaces between words.

Although kanji replace hiragana and katakana in verbs and adjectives, kanji do not replace the entirety of verbs and adjectives. If kanji replaced the entirety of verbs and adjectives, one could not read how verb and adjective endings are conjugated. As kanji do not replace the entirely of verbs and adjectives, kanji replace a portion of the stems of verbs and adjectives. The stem of a verb or adjective is the portion of the word that is not changed during conjugation. Though kanji replace a portion of the stems of verbs and adjectives, different kanji replace different portions of stems. One must memorize which hiragana or katakana of each verb or adjective stem the appropriate kanji replaces. To illustrate, consider what hiragana of the stems of the う-verbs わかる (to understand) and はなす (to speak) are replaced with the appropriate kanji. The stem of わかる is わか. The appropriate kanji 分 replaces わ, producing 分かる. While only a part of the stem of わかる is replaced with the appropriate kanji, the entire stem of はなす is replaced with the appropriate kanji. The stem はな of はなす is replaced with the appropriate kanji 話, producing 話す.

Conjugation Formula Charts

	Informal			
	Non-Past		Past	
	Affirmative	Negative	Affirmative	Negative
Basic	B3	B1 + ない	Bた	B1 + なかった
Volitional	B5	B1 + ないようにしよう	NA	NA
Presumptive	B3 + だろう	B1 + ないだろう	Bた + (だ)ろう*	B1 + なかった(だ)ろう*
Order	Bて	B1 + ない(で)*	NA	NA
Rude Order	See table A.	B3 + な	NA	NA
Obligation	B1 + なければならない	Bて + はならない	NA	NA
ば Conditional	B4 + ば	B1 + なければ	B4 + ば	B1 + なければ
たら Conditional	Bた + ら	B1 + なかったら	Bた + ら	B1 + なかったら
Colloquial Conditional	See table B.	See table B.	See table B.	See table B.
Standard Continuative	Bて; B2	B1 + ないで; B1 + なく(て)*	Bて; B2	B1 + ないで; B1 + なく(て)*
たり Continuative	Bた + り	B1 + なかったり	Bた + り	B1 + なかったり

Verbs • 35

Table A

	Rude Order Non-Past Affirmative
う-Verbs	B4
る-Verbs	Stem + ろ
する	しろ
くる	こい

Table B

	う-Verbs	る-Verbs	する	くる
Colloquial Conditional Affirmative	B2 + や	Stem + りゃ	すりゃ	くりゃ
Colloquial Conditional Negative	B1 + なきゃ	Stem + なきゃ	しなきゃ	こなきゃ

	Formal			
	Non-Past		Past	
	Affirmative	Negative	Affirmative	Negative
Basic	B2 + ます	B2 + ません	B2 + ました	B2 + ませんでした
Volitional	B2 + ましょう	B1 + ないようにしましょう	NA	NA
Presumptive	B3 + でしょう	B1 + ないでしょう	Bた + でしょう	B1 + なかったでしょう
Request	Bて + ください	B1 + ないでください	NA	NA
Order	B2 + なさい	NA	NA	NA
Obligation	B1 + なければなりません	Bて + はなりません	NA	NA
ば Conditional	B4 + ば	B1 + なければ	B4 + ば	B1 + なければ
たら Conditional	Bた + ら	B1 + なかったら	Bた + ら	B1 + なかったら
Standard Continuative	Bて; B2	B1 + ないで; B1 + なく(て)*	Bて; B2	B1 + ないで; B1 + なく(て)*
たり Continuative	Bた + り	B1 + なかったり	Bた + り	B1 + なかったり

		Informal				
		Non-Past			Past	
		Affirmative	Negative		Affirmative	Negative
Basic		たべる will eat	たべない will not eat		たべた did eat	たべなかった did not eat
Volitional		たべよう let's eat	たべないようにしよう let's not eat		NA	NA
Presumptive		たべるだろう probably will eat	たべないだろう probably will not eat		たべた(だ)ろう* probably did eat	たべなかった(だ)ろう* probably did not eat
Order		たべて eat	たべない(で)* do not eat		NA	NA
Rude Order		たべろ eat!	たべるな do not eat!		NA	NA
Obligation		たべなければならない must eat	たべてはならない must not eat		NA	NA
ば Conditional		たべれば if will eat	たべなければ if will not eat		たべれば if did eat	たべなければ if did not eat
たら Conditional		たべたら if will eat	たべなかったら if will not eat		たべたら if/when did eat	たべなかったら if/when did not eat
Colloquial Conditional		たべりや if will eat	たべなきや if will not eat		たべりや if did eat	たべなきや if did not eat
Standard Continuative		たべて; たべ will eat and	たべないで; たべなく(て)* will not eat and		たべて; たべ did eat and	たべないで; たべなく(て)* did not eat and
たり Continuative		たべたり will eat and	たべなかったり will not eat and		たべたり did eat and	たべなかったり did not eat and

38 • Japan-Ease Grammar

	Formal					
	Non-Past		Past			
	Affirmative	Negative	Affirmative	Negative		
Basic	たべます will eat	たべません will not eat	たべました did eat	たべませんでした did not eat		
Volitional	たべましょう let's eat	たべないようにしましょう let's not eat	NA	NA		
Presumptive	たべるでしょう probably will eat	たべないでしょう probably will not eat	たべたでしょう probably did eat	たべなかったでしょう probably did not eat		
Request	たべてください please eat	たべないでください please do not eat	NA	NA		
Order	たべな eat	NA	NA	NA		
Obligation	たべなければなりません must eat	たべてはなりません must not eat	NA	NA		
ば Conditional	たべれば if will eat	たべなければ if will not eat	たべれば if did eat	たべなければ if did not eat		
たら Conditional	たべたら if will eat	たべなかったら if will not eat	たべたら if/when did eat	たべなかったら if/when did not eat		
Standard Continuative	たべて; たべ will eat and	たべないで、たべなく(て)* will not eat and	たべて; たべ did eat and	たべないで、たべなく(て)* did not eat and		
たり Continuative	たべたり will eat and	たべなかったり will not eat and	たべたり did eat and	たべなかったり did not eat and		

*The hiragana in parentheses are normally included; the verbs are colloquial when the hiragana in parentheses are omitted. For example, the hiragana て in the informal order non-past negative formula B1 + ない(て) is normally included. The verb たべる (to eat) conjugated according to this formula B1 + ない(て) is たべない(て) (do not eat). That being the case, たべいって, which does include て, is more common than たべない, which does not include て.

Verbs • 39

Example Sentence Charts

Informal		
Form	Placement	Example Sentence
Basic	Sentence End	こうじょう・で・は・コンピュータ・の・チップ・を・つくる。[45] The factory manufactures computer chips.
Volitional	Sentence End	スカイプ・で・しゃべろう。[46] Let's chat over Skype.
Presumptive	Sentence End	わたし・は・8(はち)・じ・まで・に・イベント・に・とうちゃくするだろう。[47] I will probably arrive at the event by 8 o'clock.
Order	Sentence End	おきて。[48] Wake up.
Rude Order	Sentence End	はなすな。[49] Don't talk!
Obligation	Sentence End	かれ・は・いしゃ・に・いかなければならない。[50] He must go to the doctor.
ば Conditional	Mid-Sentence	やちん・は・ユーティリティ・を・ふくめば、たかくない。[51] If the rent includes utilities, it is not expensive
たら Conditional	Mid-Sentence	ゆめ・を・あきらめたら、ざんねんだ。[52] If you give up on your dreams, it would be a pity.
Colloquial Conditional	Mid-Sentence	それ・を・すりゃ、こうかいする。[53] If you do that, you will regret it.
Standard Continuative	Mid-Sentence	わたし・は・かれ・に・あって、ひとめぼれだった。[54] I met him and it was love at first sight.
たり Continuative	Mid-Sentence	わたしたち・は・テレビ・を・みたり、トランプ・を・したり・した。[55] We watched television and played cards (in addition to other activities).

---

45 こうじょう factory • コンピュータ computer • チップ chip • つくる to make (う-verb)
46 スカイプ Skype • しゃべる to chat (う-verb)
47 わたし I • はち 8 • じ hour • イベント event • とうちゃくする to arrive (する-verb)
48 おきる to wake up (る-verb)
49 はなす to talk (う-verb)
50 かれ he • いしゃ doctor • いく to go (う-verb)
51 やちん rent • ユーティリティ utilities • ふくむ to include (う-verb) • たかい expensive
52 ゆめ dream • あきらめる to give up (る-verb) • ざんねんな deplorable
53 それ that • する to do (irregular verb) • こうかいする to regret (する-verb)
54 わたし I • かれ he • あう to meet (う-verb) • ひとめぼれ love at first sight
55 わたしたち we • テレビ television • みる to watch (る-verb) • トランプ playing cards • する to do (irregular verb)

		Formal	
Form	Placement	Example Sentence	
Basic	Sentence End	その・かいしゃ・は・コーヒー・まめ・を・ゆしゅつします。[56] That company exports coffee beans.	
Volitional	Sentence End	こうぎ・を・はじめましょう。[57] Let's begin the lecture.	
Presumptive	Sentence End	あした・ゆき・が・ふるでしょう。[58] It will probably snow tomorrow.	
Request	Sentence End	ちょうぞう・に・て・を・ふれないでください。[59] Please don't touch the statue.	
Order	Sentence End	ジャケット・を・きなさい。[60] Wear a jacket.	
Obligation	Sentence End	がくせい・は・べんきょうしなければなりません。[61] Students must study.	
ば Conditional	Mid-Sentence	かかく・が・さがれば、わたし・は・かいます。[62] If the price decreases, I'll buy it.	
たら Conditional	Mid-Sentence	これ・を・かりたら、かえしてください。[63] If you borrow this, please return it.	
Standard Continuative	Mid-Sentence	はた・が・あがって、しみん・は・こっか・を・うたいました。[64] The flag rose and the citizens sang the national anthem.	
たり Continuative	Mid-Sentence	そうじ・の・ひと・は・ゴミ・を・だしたり、モップ・で・ゆか・を・そうじしたり・します。[65] The janitor takes out the trash and cleans the floor with a mop (in addition to other activities).	

---

56 その that • かいしゃ company • コーヒー coffee • まめ bean • ゆしゅつする to export (する-verb)
57 こうぎ lecture • はじめる to begin (る-verb)
58 あした tomorrow • ゆき snow • ふる to fall (う-verb)
59 ちょうぞう statue • て hand • ふれる to touch (る-verb)
60 ジャケット jacket • きる to wear (る-verb)
61 がくせい student • べんきょうする to study (する-verb)
62 かかく price • さがる to go down (う-verb) • わたし I • かう to buy (う-verb)
63 これ this • かりる to borrow (る-verb) • かえす to return (う-verb)
64 はた flag • あがる to rise (う-verb) • しみん citizen • こっか national anthem • うたう to sing (う-verb)
65 そうじ cleaning • ひと person • ゴミ trash • だす to take out (う-verb) • モップ mop • ゆか floor • そうじする to clean (する-verb) • する to do (irregular verb)

Conditional Verbs

The non-past affirmative and past affirmative formulas in the respective conditional rows are the same. For example, both the formal ば conditional non-past affirmative formula and formal ば conditional past affirmative formula are B4 + ば.

Similar to the way in which the non-past affirmative and past affirmative formulas are the same, the non-past negative and past negative formulas in the respective conditional rows are the same. For example, both the formal ば conditional non-past negative formula and formal ば conditional past negative formula are B1 + なければ.

Because the non-past affirmative and past affirmative formulas are the same, and the non-past negative and past negative formulas are the same, ば conditional, たら conditional, and colloquial conditional verbs are in non-past instead of past tense unless otherwise indicated by context. For example, because context does not indicate otherwise, the ば conditional verb ねれば is in non-past tense in the sentence わたし・は・もっと・ねれば、つかれないだろう (if I sleep more, I probably won't be tired). As a non-past tense verb, ねれば means "if sleep" instead of "if had slept."[66]

Although ねれば is in non-past tense in the sentence わたし・は・もっと・ねれば、つかれないだろう, context indicates that ねれば is in past tense in the sentence わたし・は・もっと・ねれば、つかれなかっただろう (if I had slept more, I probably wouldn't have been tired). This context results from the clause つかれなかっただろう. The clause つかれなかっただろう is in past tense because つかれなかっただろう (probably wouldn't have been tired) is the verb つかれる conjugated according to the past formula B1 + なかっただろう. As the clause つかれなかっただろう is in past tense, ねれば is in past tense. In other words, ねれば means "if had slept" instead of "if sleep."

When a たら conditional verb is in past tense, the meaning of the verb may mean "if did/did not do the verb" or "when did/did not do the verb," depending on context. For example, context indicates that あらったら, which is the verb あらう (to wash) conjugated according to the たら conditional

---

[66] わたし I • もっと more • ねる to sleep (る-verb) •
つかれる to become tired (る-verb)

affirmative formula Bた + ら, is not conditional in the sentence ジーンズ・を・あらったら、いろ・が・にじみました (when I washed the jeans, the color ran). This context results from the clause いろ・が・にじみました (the color ran). The verb にじむ (to run) in this clause is conjugated according to the basic formula B2 + ました rather than the presumptive formula Bた + でしょう. As such, the clause いろ・が・にじみました means "the color ran" instead of "the color probably would have run."[67]

Although a ば conditional, たら conditional, or colloquial conditional verb can create a conditional past tense phrase, a verb can also form a conditional past tense phrase by modifying the noun ばあい (meaning "case"), thereby creating a relative clause. As explained in the relative clause section of this book, informal basic verbs can modify nouns. Since たべた is the verb たべる (to eat) conjugated according to the informal basic formula Bた, たべた can modify the noun ばあい. The relative clause たべた・ばあい literally translates as "case that ate" but means "if ate."

A relative clause that contains a modifying verb and the modified noun ばあい ends a mid-sentence clause, instead of a sentence, like ば conditional, たら conditional, and colloquial conditional verbs do. For example, the relative clause いぬ・が・あれ・を・たべた・ばあい (if the dog ate that), which contains the modifying verb たべた and the modified noun ばあい, ends the mid-sentence clause in the sentence いぬ・が・あれ・を・たべた・ばあい・は、びょうきに・なります. The sentence いぬ・が・あれ・を・たべた・ばあい・は、びょうきに・なります literally translates to "as for the case that the dog ate that, it would become sick," but means "if the dog ate that, then it would become sick."[68]

Continuative Verbs

Standard continuative verbs mean "do/do not/did/did not do the verb and." For example, in the sentence わたし・は・しょく・を・うしなって、き・が・おもい

---

67 ジーンズ jeans • あらう to wash (う-verb) • いろ color • にじむ to run (color) (う-verb)

68 いぬ dog • あれ that • たべる to eat (る-verb) • ばあい case • びょうきな sick • なる to become (う-verb)

です (I lost my job and am heavy-hearted), うしなって, which is the verb うしなう (to lose) conjugated according to the standard continuative affirmative formula Bて, means "lost and."[69]

Each standard continuative affirmative cell contains two formulas. These formulas are Bて and B2. Standard continuative affirmative formula Bて is used more often than standard continuative affirmative formula B2. Because Bて is used more often than B2, Bて is listed before B2 in the standard continuative affirmative cells.

Like each standard continuative affirmative cell, each standard continuative negative cell contains two formulas. These two standard continuative negative formulas are B1 + ないで and B1 + なく(て). Standard continuative negative formula B1 + ないで is used more often than standard continuative negative formula B1 + なく(て). Because B1 + ないで is used more often than B1 + なくて, B1 + ないで is listed before B1 + なく(て) in the standard continuative negative cells.

Unlike standard continuative verbs, たり continuative verbs can indicate that a list is incomplete. In other words, たり continuative verbs can indicate that other actions are applicable to the list. For example, the sentence ひしょ・は・でんわ・に・でたり、ミーティング・を・スケジュールしたり・します (the secretary does such things as answering the telephone and scheduling meetings) contains でたり, which is the verb でる (to answer) conjugated according to the たり continuative affirmative formula Bた + り. The sentence also contains スケジュールしたり, which is the verb スケジュールする (to schedule) conjugated according to the たり continuative affirmative formula Bた + り. As たり continuative verbs, でたり and スケジュールしたり indicate that activities in addition to answering the telephone and scheduling meetings are applicable to the list and that the secretary has other duties.[70]

While in some instances たり continuative verbs indicate an incomplete list, in other instances たり continuative verbs mean "in some instances

---

69 わたし I • しょく employment • うしなう to part with (う-verb) • き heart • おもい heavy

70 ひしょ secretary • でんわ telephone • でる to answer (the telephone) (る-verb) • ミーティング meeting • スケジュールする to schedule (する-verb) • する to do (irregular verb)

do/do not/did/did not do the verb." For example, in the sentence わたし・は・シャワー・を・あびたり、おふろ・に・はいったり・する, あびたり, which is the verb あびる (to take [a shower]) conjugated according to the たり continuative affirmative formula Bた + り, means "in some instances take [a shower]." Likewise, はいったり, which is the verb はいる (to enter [the bath]) conjugated according to the たり continuative affirmative formula Bた + り, means "in some instances enter [the bath]." Given these points, the sentence literally translates as "I in some instances take a shower and in some instances enter the bath" and means "sometimes I take a shower and sometimes I take a bath."[71]

All verbs creating a たり continuative list should be in たり continuative form. For example, in the sentence わたし・は・シャワー・を・あびたり、おふろ・に・はいたり・する, the verbs あびたり and はいたり that create the list are in たり continuative form. Likewise, in the sentence ひしょ・は・でんわ・に・でたり、ミーティング・を・スケジュールしたり・します, the verbs でたり and スケジュールしたり that create the list are in たり continuative form.

Although all verbs creating a たり continuative list should be in たり continuative form, a たり continuative verb cannot end a sentence. As the example sentence charts indicate, たり continuative verbs are placed mid-sentence rather than at the end of sentences. Since a たり continuative verb cannot end a sentence, a conjugation of the verb する ends the sentences わたし・は・シャワー・を・あびたり、おふろ・に・はいたり・する and ひしょ・は・でんわ・に・でたり、ミーティング・を・スケジュールしたり・します.

Volitional Verbs

The informal volitional non-past negative formula is B1 + ないようにしよう. This formula B1 + ないようにしよう consists of B1 + ない, ように and しよう. The first component B1 + ない is the informal basic non-past negative formula, which means "will not do the verb." The second component ように is an expression that means "in order to." The third component しよう (let's do)

---

71   わたし I • シャワー shower • あびる to take (a shower) • おふろ bath • はいる to enter (う-verb) • する to do (irregular verb)

is the irregular verb する (to do) conjugated according to the informal volitional non-past affirmative formula B5 (meaning "let's do the verb"). Given these points, B1 + ない + ように + しよう literally translates as "let's do in order to not do the verb." For example, あわてないようにしよう, which is the verb あわてる (to panic) conjugated according to the formula B1 + ないようにしよう, literally translates as "let's do in order to not panic."

Although B1 + ないようにしよう literally translates as "let's do in order to not do the verb," B1 + ないようにしよう means "let's not do the verb." For example, あわてないようにしよう, which is the verb あわてる (to panic) conjugated according to the formula B1 + ないようにしよう, means "let's not panic."

Whereas B1 + ないようにしよう (let's not do the verb) is the *informal* volitional non-past negative formula, the *formal* volitional non-past negative formula is B1 + ないようにしましょう (let's not do the verb). The informal volitional non-past negative formula B1 + ないようにしよう contains しよう (let's do), which is the verb する (to do) conjugated according to the *informal* volitional non-past affirmative formula B5, and the formal volitional non-past negative formula B1 + ないようにしましょう contains しましょう (let's do), which is the verb する conjugated according to the *formal* volitional non-past affirmative formula B2 + ましょう.

Obligation Verbs

The informal obligation non-past affirmative formula is B1 + なければならない (must do the verb). This formula B1 + なければならない is a combination of the ば conditional negative formula B1 + なければ (meaning "if will not do the verb") and ならない. ならない (will not become) is the verb なる (to become) conjugated according to the informal basic non-past negative formula B1 + ない. As a result, B1 + なければならない literally translates as "if will not do the verb, will not become." For example, いそがなければならない, which is the verb いそぐ (to hurry) conjugated according to the formula B1 + なければならない, literally translates as "if will not hurry, will not become."

Although B1 + なければならない literally translates as "if will not do the verb, will not become," B1 + なければならない means "must do the verb." For example, いそがなければならない, which is the verb いそぐ (to hurry) conjugated according to the formula B1 + なければならない, means "must hurry."

Whereas B1 + なければならない (must do the verb) is the *informal* obligation non-past affirmative formula, the *formal* obligation non-past affirmative formula is B1 + なければなりません (must do the verb). The informal formula B1 + なければならない contains ならない (will not become), which is the verb なる (to become) conjugated according to the *informal* basic non-past negative formula B1 + ない, and the formal formula B1 + なければなりません contains なりません (will not become), which is the verb なる conjugated according to the *formal* basic non-past negative formula B2 + ません.

Basic Verbs

The informal basic negative formulas may be followed by です. The informal basic negative formulas are the informal basic non-past negative formula B1 + ない (will not do the verb) and the informal basic past negative formula B1 + なかった (did not do the verb). As です may follow these formulas, B1 + ないです (will not do the verb) and B1 + なかったです (did not do the verb) are permitted formulas. To illustrate, the verb ほす (to dry) can be conjugated according to the formula B1 + ないです to obtain ほさないです (will not dry), or according to the formula B1 + なかったです to obtain ほさなっかたです (did not dry).

When followed by です, the informal basic negative formulas become formal. In other words, B1 + ないです and B1 + なかったです are respectively interchangeable with B2 + ません (will not do the verb) and B2 + ませんでした (did not do the verb). B1 + ないです and B1 + なかったです are rarely used so these formulas are not included in the formal verb formula chart.

Exceptional Verb ある

ある (meaning "to exist") is an exceptional verb. As ある is an う-verb, and the B1 formula for an う-verb that ends in る in B3 is 〜(あ), one may assume that the B1 of ある is あら. However, ある is a special case and no B1 of ある exists.

Therefore, ある cannot be conjugated according to the formulas containing B1 in the verb formula charts.

When ある cannot be conjugated according to a formula containing B1, one substitutes ある with the い-adjective ない (meaning "nonexistent"). One then conjugates ない according to the appropriate formula in the い-adjective formula charts.

How does one select the appropriate い-adjective formula when conjugating ない? Because ない is an い-adjective with a negative meaning, ない is conjugated according to a negative い-adjective formula to obtain an affirmative meaning. To illustrate, ある cannot be conjugated according to the informal obligation non-past affirmative formula B1 + なければならない (must do the verb) that contains B1. To obtain an informal obligation non-past *affirmative* meaning, ない is conjugated according to the informal obligation non-past *negative* い-adjective formula stem + くてはならない (must not be the い-adjective). Because the stem of ない is な, なくてはならない is ない conjugated according to the formula stem + くてはならない. なくてはならない contains a double negative. Although the literal translation of なくてはならない is "must not be nonexistent," なくてはならない means "must exist."

The only affirmative formula in the verb formula charts that contains B1 besides the informal obligation non-past affirmative formula B1 + なければならない (must do the verb) is the formal obligation non-past affirmative formula B1 + なければなりません (must do the verb). Since ある cannot be conjugated according to the formal obligation non-past affirmative formula B1 + なければなりません (must do the verb) because it contains B1, ない is conjugated to obtain the formal obligation non-past affirmative meaning of ある. To obtain a formal obligation non-past *affirmative* meaning, ない is conjugated according to the formal obligation non-past *negative* い-adjective formula stem + くてはなりません (must not be the い-adjective). ない conjugated according to the formula stem + くてはなりません is なくてはなりません. Although the literal translation of なくてはなりません is "must not be nonexistent," なくてはなりません means "must exist."

Similar to the manner in which ない is conjugated according to negative い-adjective formulas to obtain an affirmative meaning, ない is conjugated according to affirmative い-adjective formulas to retain a negative meaning. To demonstrate, ある cannot be conjugated according to the informal たり

continuative non-past negative formula B1 + なかったり (does not do the verb and) that contains B1. To obtain an informal たり continuative non-past *negative* meaning, ない is conjugated according to the informal たり continuative non-past *affirmative* い-adjective formula stem + かったり (is the い-adjective and). Because the stem of ない is な, ない conjugated according to the formula stem + かったり is なかったり (nonexistent and).

Knowing how ある is conjugated is not only necessary for conjugating ある as an independent verb, it is also necessary for understanding how ある-copulas are formed. Affirmative ある-copulas are made up of で (the beginning of affirmative ある-copulas) and a conjugation of ある. In a like manner, negative ある-copulas are made up of で, では, or じゃ (the beginnings of negative ある-copulas), and a conjugation of ある. The form of ある that corresponds to the form of the ある-copula is employed. For example, the *informal basic past affirmative* ある-copula であった contains the *informal basic past affirmative* form of ある, which is あった. As another example, the *informal presumptive past negative* ある-copula でなかった(だ)ろう contains the *informal presumptive past negative* form of ある, which is なかった(だ)ろう.

Advanced Conjugations

The tables below indicate how to obtain the B3 of potential, causative, passive, and causative passive verbs. For instance, it is shown below that the formula for obtaining the potential B3 of an う-verb is B4 + る (to be able to do the verb). To demonstrate, はこべる (to be able to carry), which is the う-verb はこぶ (to carry) conjugated according to the formula B4 + る, is a potential B3.

How is a potential, causative, passive, or causative passive B3 conjugated? When a verb becomes potential, causative, passive, or causative passive, the verb type (whether a verb is an う-verb or る-verb) is determined by the ending of the potential, causative, passive, or causative passive B3. For example, はこべる (to be able to carry), which is the potential B3 of はこぶ (to carry), ends in 〜(え)る like a る-verb. Thus, はこべる is a る-verb even though はこぶ is an う-verb. Since はこべる is a る-verb, the bases of はこべる are obtained according to the る-verb base formulas. For example, the B2 of はこべる is はこべ because the る-verb B2 formula is stem.

Because the verb type is determined by the ending of a potential, causative, passive, or causative passive B3, the irregular verbs する and くる become う-verbs or る-verbs in potential, causative, passive, and causative passive form. In other words, する and くる do not conjugate as exceptional verbs in potential, causative, passive, and causative passive form. For example, させられる (to be made to do), which is the causative passive B3 of the irregular verb する (to do), is a る-verb because of the 〜(え)る ending. In other words, させられる conjugates as a る-verb even though する is an irregular verb.

	う-Verbs	る-Verbs
Potential B3	B4 + る	Stem + られる; Stem + れる*
Causative B3	B1 + せる; B1 + す*	Stem + させる; Stem + さす*
Passive B3	B1 + れる	Stem + られる
Causative Passive B3	B1 + せられる; B1 + される*	Stem + させられる

	Example Using う-Verb はらう (to pay)	Example Using る-Verb こたえる (to answer)
Potential B3	はらえる to be able to pay	こたえられる; こたえれる* to be able to answer
Causative B3	はらわせる; はらわす* to make/let pay	こたえさせる; こたえさす* to make/let answer
Passive B3	はらわれる to be paid	こたえられる to be answered
Causative Passive B3	はらわせられる; はらわされる* to be made to pay	こたえさせられる to be made to answer

	Irregular Verbs	
	する	くる
Potential B3	できる to be able to do	こられる; これる* to be able to come
Causative B3	させる; さす* to make/let do	こさせる; こさす* to make/let come
Passive B3	される to be done	こられる to be approached
Causative Passive B3	させられる to be made to do	こさせられる to be made to come

*The shorter forms indicated by an asterisk are colloquial. These colloquial forms can be informal or formal depending on whether the colloquial B3 is conjugated according to an informal or formal formula in the verb formula charts.

Advanced Conjugations and Particle Use

A noun particle assigns a noun a role (such as topic, subject, or indirect object) in a sentence, as explained later in the particle appendix. For example, the indirect object particle に marks a noun as the indirect object of a sentence.

Although a noun particle assigns nouns a role, the function of a role may differ in a sentence with a potential verb, a sentence with a causative verb, a sentence with a passive verb, a sentence with a causative passive verb, and a sentence with a regular verb (a verb that is not potential, causative, passive, or causative passive). For example, although the indirect object particle に marks nouns as indirect objects, the function of an indirect object differs in a sentence with a causative verb, a sentence with a passive verb, a sentence with a causative passive verb, and a sentence with a verb that is not causative, passive, or causative passive.

To illustrate how the function of a role may differ, consider a sentence with a regular verb and a sentence with a causative verb. As a regular verb means "to do the verb," the topic of a regular verb is the noun that does the verb. Conversely, the indirect object of a regular verb is the noun that is the recipient of the verb. For example, in the sentence わたし・は・むすめ・に・パッケージ・を・ゆうそうする (I will mail a package to my daughter), which contains the regular verb ゆうそうする (will mail), the topic わたし (I) does the verb (mails). The indirect object むすめ (daughter) is the recipient of the verb (mailing).[72]

In a sentence with a causative verb, the topic function differs and the indirect object function differs. As a causative verb means "to make/let do the verb," the topic of a causative verb is the noun that makes or lets the indirect object do the verb. The indirect object is the noun that is made or allowed to do the verb. For example, in the sentence りょうしん・は・こども・に・ピアノ・を・ならわせる (the parents make the child learn piano), which contains the causative verb ならわせる (make learn), the topic りょうしん (parents) makes the indirect object こども (child) do the verb (learn). The indirect object こども (child) is made to do the verb (learn).[73]

For more information regarding how the functions of noun particles differ with a regular verb, potential verb, causative verb, passive verb, and causative passive verb, see the particle appendix.

Stem + られる Formula

Both the formula for obtaining the passive B3 of a る-verb and the formula for obtaining the non-colloquial potential B3 of a る-verb are stem + られる. As a result, the passive B3 and non-colloquial potential B3 of a る-verb are the same. For example, the passive B3 and non-colloquial potential B3 of the る-verb たべる are たべられる. In other words, たべられる means both "to be eaten" and "to be able to eat."

Because the formulas for obtaining the passive B3 and non-colloquial potential B3 of a る-verb are the same, readers and listeners need to determine whether stem + られる verbs are potential or passive.

---

[72] わたし I • むすめ daughter • パッケージ package • ゆうそうする to mail (する-verb)

[73] りょうしん parents • こども child • ピアノ piano • ならう to learn (う-verb)

Context indicates whether a stem + られる verb is potential or passive. For example, in the following passage consider how context from the first sentence indicates whether the stem + られる verb in the second sentence is potential or passive: その・せいじか・は・わいろ・を・うけとりました。かれ・は・しらべられました。 The first sentence その・せいじか・は・わいろ・を・うけとりました means "that politician accepted bribes." The second sentence かれ・は・しらべられました contains しらべられました, which is the verb しらべる (to investigate) conjugated according to the B3 formula stem + られる, and then conjugated according to the formal basic past affirmative formula B2 + ました that means "did the verb." If しらべられました is passive, what does the second sentence mean? A passive verb means "to have the verb done to one." Thus, しらべられました means "was investigated" if passive. How does the phrase "was investigated" relate to the noun かれ (he) that is marked with topic particle は? Topic particle は indicates that the topic of the sentence is かれ. (For information about particles, see the particle section of this book.) The topic of a passive verb is the noun that the verb is done to. Hence, the verb is done to the topic かれ. That is to say, he is investigated. To be brief, if しらべられました is passive, the sentence かれ・は・しらべられました means "he was investigated."[74]

On the other hand, what does the sentence かれ・は・しらべられました mean if しらべられました is potential instead of passive? A potential verb means "to be able to do the verb." Accordingly, しらべられました means "could investigate" if potential. How does the phrase "could investigate" relate to the topic かれ? The topic of a potential verb is the noun that can do the verb. Therefore, the topic かれ can do the verb. In other words, he can investigate. In short, if しらべられました is potential, the sentence かれ・は・しらべられました means "he could investigate."

Compare the translation "he could investigate," which supposes that しらべられました is potential, with the translation "he was investigated," which supposes that しらべられました is passive. What is the intended meaning? Context from the previous sentence その・せいじか・は・わいろ・を・うけとりました (that politician accepted bribes) indicates that the politician would be investigated, rather than investigate.

74　その that • せいじか politician • わいろ bribe • うけとる to accept (う-verb) • かれ he • しらべる to investigate (る-verb)

VERB AUXILIARIES

Each verb auxiliary connects to a particular base. Case in point, the verb auxiliary みる connects to Bて to form the verb base + verb auxiliary phrase Bて + みる. Bて + みる means "to try to do the verb." For example, the verb ねる (to sleep) conjugated according to Bて + みる is ねてみる (to try to sleep).

Like the verb auxiliary みる, the verb auxiliary いる connects to Bて. Bて + いる is a progressive form that means "to be doing the verb." For instance, the verb ねる (to sleep) conjugated according to Bて + いる is ねている (to be sleeping).

While the verb auxiliary いる connects to Bて, the verb auxiliary ながら connects to B2. B2 + ながら means "while doing the verb." As an illustration, ねながら (while sleeping) is the verb ねる (to sleep) conjugated according to B2 + ながら.

Like the verb auxiliary ながら, the verb auxiliary たい connects to B2. B2 + たい means "to want to do the verb." To demonstrate, the verb ねる (to sleep) conjugated according to B2 + たい is ねたい (to want to sleep).

Many verb base + verb auxiliary phrases can be conjugated. During conjugation, one does not change the base of the verb that connects to the verb auxiliary. Rather, one conjugates the verb auxiliary. To illustrate, consider how to conjugate the verb base + verb auxiliary phrase B2 + たい (meaning "to want to do the verb"). To conjugate B2 + たい, one conjugates the verb auxiliary たい. たい conjugates like an い-adjective. In other words, たい is conjugated according to the い-adjective formulas. Accordingly, たい can be conjugated according to the い-adjective formal basic non-past negative formula stem +

55

くないです meaning "not the い-adjective" to obtain たくないです. When たい is swapped with たくないです in the verb base + verb auxiliary phrase B2 + たい, one acquires B2 + たくないです. B2 + たくないです means "do not want to do the verb." For example, the verb いく (to go) conjugated according to the verb base + verb auxiliary phrase B2 + たくないです is いきたくないです (do not want to go). いきたくないです is used in the sentence わたし・は・いきたくないです (I do not want to go).[75]

As another example of how verb base + verb auxiliary phrases are conjugated, take the verb base + verb auxiliary phrase Bて + みる (meaning "to try to do the verb"). To conjugate Bて + みる, one conjugates the verb auxiliary みる. The verb auxiliary みる is a verb. Therefore, みる is conjugated according to the verb formulas. For example, みる can be conjugated according to the informal ば conditional non-past affirmative formula B4 + ば meaning "if will do the verb" to obtain みれば. When みる is swapped with みれば in the verb base + verb auxiliary phrase Bて + みる, one acquires Bて + みれば. Bて + みれば means "if will try to do the verb." For example, the verb やる (to do) conjugated according to the verb base + verb auxiliary phrase Bて + みれば is やってみれば (if try to do). This phrase is used in the sentence やってみれば、せいこうする (if you try to do it, you will succeed).[76]

Some verb base + verb auxiliary phrases cannot be conjugated. For example, the verb base + verb auxiliary phrase B2 + ながら (which means "while doing the verb") cannot be conjugated to create phrases such as "while not doing the verb" and "if while doing the verb."

Although some verb base + verb auxiliary phrases cannot be conjugated, it is still possible to create phrases that mean what inflections of the verb base + verb auxiliary phrases would mean. For instance, even though the verb base + verb auxiliary phrase B2 + ながら (meaning "while doing the verb") cannot be conjugated to create phrases such as "while not doing the verb" and "if while doing the verb," it is still possible to create phrases such as "while not doing the verb" and "if while doing the verb." For example, Bて + いない・とき・に means "while not during the verb."

---

75   わたし I • いく to go (う-verb)
76   やる to do (う-verb) • せいこうする to succeed (する-verb)

How is the relative clause Bて + いない・とき created? The relative clause Bて + いない・とき contains an inflection of the verb base + verb auxiliary phrase Bて + いる. As mentioned earlier, the verb base + verb auxiliary phrase Bて + いる is a progressive form meaning "to be doing the verb." Because the verb auxiliary いる is a verb, いる is conjugated according to verb formulas. いる conjugated according to the informal basic non-past negative formula B1 + ない (meaning "does not do the verb") is いない. Replacing いる with いない in the verb base + verb auxiliary phrase Bて + いる (meaning "doing the verb") produces Bて + いない (meaning "not doing the verb"). As stated in the relative clause chapter, informal basic verbs can modify a noun to form a relative clause. Because the verb auxiliary いない is the verb いる conjugated according to the informal basic formula B1 + ない, いない is an informal basic verb. Consequently, Bて + いない can modify a noun to create a relative clause. いない modifies the noun とき (meaning "time") in the relative clause Bて + いない・とき. Bて + いない・とき・に literally translates as "at the time that is not doing the verb" but means "while not doing the verb." To illustrate, the sentence わたし・が・ちゅうい・を・はらっていない・とき・に、だれか・が・わたし・の・かばん・を・ぬすみました, which contains Bて + いない・とき・に, literally translates as "at the time that I was not paying attention, someone stole my bag" but means "while I was not paying attention, someone stole my bag."[77]

---

[77] わたし I • ちゅうい attention • はらう to pay (う-verb) • とき time • だれか somebody • かばん bag • ぬすむ to steal (う-verb)

RELATIVE CLAUSES

Exceptions aside, the informal basic forms of a verb, adjective or copula can modify a noun, thereby creating a relative clause.

Relative Clauses with a Modifying Verb

Examples:
のむ・ひと
person who will drink

のまない・ひと
person who will not drink

のんだ・ひと
person who drank

のまなかった・ひと[78]
person who did not drink

---

78 のむ to drink (う-verb) • ひと person

Relative Clauses with a Modifying い-Adjective

Examples:
>むずかしい・テスト
>test that is difficult
>
>むずかしくない・テスト
>test that is not difficult
>
>むずかしかった・テスト
>test that was difficult
>
>むずかしくなかった・テスト[79]
>test that was not difficult

Relative Clauses with a Modifying な-Adjective

Examples:
>ゆうめいな・やくしゃ
>actor that is famous
>
>ゆうめいでない・やくしゃ
>actor that is not famous
>
>ゆうめいだった・やくしゃ
>actor that was famous
>
>ゆうめいでなかった・やくしゃ[80]
>actor that was not famous

There is an exception to the rule that the informal basic forms of な-adjectives modify nouns. Although stem + だ is an informal basic non-past affirmative form of な-adjectives, stem + だ does not modify nouns. For example, ていねいだ・うけつけがかり (receptionist who is polite), which contains the stem + だ form of the な-adjective ていねいな (polite), is grammatically incorrect. Instead

---

79 むずかしい difficult • テスト test
80 ゆうめいな famous • やくしゃ actor

of stem + だ, modifying non-past affirmative な-adjectives usually use dictionary form. For example, the relative clause ていねいな・うけつけがかり (receptionist who is polite), which contains the dictionary form of the な-adjective ていねいな, is grammatically correct.[81]

Like stem + だ, stem + である is an informal basic non-past affirmative form of な-adjectives. Stem + である rarely modifies nouns. As previously mentioned, modifying non-past affirmative な-adjectives usually use dictionary form.

Like stem + である, stem + であった rarely modifies nouns. As the informal basic past affirmative forms of な-adjectives are stem + であった and stem + だった, modifying past affirmative な-adjectives usually use stem + だった instead.

Relative Clauses with the Modifying い-Adjective おおきい, おかしい, or ちいさい

おおきい (large), おかしい (funny), and ちいさい (small) possess an exception to the rule that the informal basic forms of い-adjectives modify nouns. Although stem + な is not an informal basic form of い-adjectives, dictionary form and stem + な can both be used to modify nouns when these exceptional い-adjectives are non-past affirmative. (Normally, when modifying い-adjectives are non-past affirmative, only dictionary form can modify nouns.) For example, the relative clause おおきな・きぼう (large hope), which contains the stem + な form of おおきい, and the relative clause おおきい・いぬ (large dog), which contains the dictionary form of おおきい, are both grammatically correct.[82]

Dictionary form and stem + な should modify different types of nouns. Dictionary form should modify tangible nouns. For example, the dictionary form おおきい modifies the tangible noun いぬ (dog) in the relative clause おおきい・いぬ (large dog). While dictionary form should modify tangible nouns, stem + な should modify intangible nouns. For example, the stem +

81　ていねいな polite • うけつけがかり receptionist
82　きぼう hope • いぬ dog

な form おおきな modifies the intangible noun きぼう (hope) in the relative clause おおきな・きぼう (large hope).

Although stem + な should modify intangible nouns and dictionary form should modify tangible nouns, the Japanese do not strictly adhere to this grammar rule. In actuality, dictionary form commonly modifies both tangible nouns and intangible nouns, and stem + な commonly modifies both tangible nouns and intangible nouns. For example, the relative clauses おおきい・いぬ (large dog) and おおきい・きぼう (large hope), in which dictionary form respectively modifies a tangible noun and intangible noun, are both common phrases.

Although the stem + な form of おおきい, おかしい, and ちいさい can modify nouns, おおきい, おかしい, and ちいさい are conjugated like normal い-adjectives when おおきい, おかしい, and ちいさい do not modify nouns. See the adjective chapter of this book for information regarding い-adjective conjugations.

Relative Clauses with a Modifying Noun

Examples:
おかねもち・の・ひと
person who is rich

おかねもちでない・ひと
person who is not rich

おかねもちだった・ひと
person who was rich

おかねもちではなかった・ひと[83]
person who was not rich

There is an exception to the rule that the informal basic copulas follow modifying nouns. Although だ is an informal basic non-past affirmative copula, だ does not follow modifying non-past affirmative nouns. For example, コメディーだ・ぎきょく(play that is a comedy), in which だ follows the modifying

---

83 おかねもち rich • ひと person

noun コメディー, is grammatically incorrect. Instead of だ, the connective particle の usually follows modifying non-past affirmative nouns. (For information regarding connective particle の, see the particle appendix.) For example, the relative clause コメディー・の・ぎきょく (play that is a comedy), in which の follows the modifying noun コメディー, is grammatically correct.[84]

Like だ, である is an informal basic non-past affirmative copula. である does not usually follow modify non-past affirmative nouns. As mentioned earlier, connective particle の usually follows modifying non-past affirmative nouns.

Like である, であった rarely follows modifying nouns. As the informal basic past affirmative copulas are であった and だった, だった usually follows modifying past affirmative nouns instead.

Relative Clauses with a Modifying Informal Obligation Form of a Verb, Adjective, or Copula

The informal obligation forms of verbs, adjectives, and copulas also modify nouns. To illustrate, the informal obligation non-past affirmative copula でなければならない (must be) modifies the noun だいがくせい (college student) to create the relative clause フルタイム・の・じゅうぎょういんでなければならない・だいがくせい (college student who must be a full time employee). This relative clause is used in the sentence フルタイム・の・じゅうぎょういんでなければならない・だいがくせい・は、しゅくだい・を・する・じかん・が・ありませんでした (the college student, who had to be a full time employee, didn't have time to do homework).[85]

As another example of how informal obligation verbs, adjectives, and copulas modify nouns, consider how a verb conjugated according to the informal obligation non-past affirmative formula B1 + なければならない can modify a noun. The verb かう (to buy) conjugated according to this formula B1 +

---

84   コメディー comedy • ぎきょく play
85   フルタイム full time • じゅうぎょういん employee • だいがくせい college student • しゅくだい homework • する to do (irregular verb) • じかん time • ある to have (う-verb)

なければならない is かわなければならない (must buy). かわなければならない modifies the noun きょうかしょ (textbook) to create the relative clause わたし・が・かわなければならない・きょうかしょ (the textbook that I must buy). This relative clause is contained in the sentence わたし・が・かわなければならない・きょうかしょ・は・たかいです (the textbook that I must buy is expensive).[86]

Why can informal obligation verbs, adjectives, and copulas modify nouns? All informal obligation verbs, adjectives, and copulas end in ならない. ならない is the verb なる conjugated according to the informal basic formula B1 + ない. As previously stated in this chapter, informal basic verbs can modify nouns. Thus, ならない can modify nouns, and so can informal obligation verbs, adjectives and copulas.

Extended Relative Clauses

Relative clauses can contain more words than the verb, adjective, or noun that immediately precedes the modified noun, and the modified noun. Words can be added before the verb, adjective, or noun immediately preceding the modified noun. In other words, a modifying phrase can be used instead of a modifying verb, adjective, or noun. For example, the modifying phrase ちこくして・あかしんごう・を・むしした (was late and disregarded [ran] a red light) is used in the extended relative clause ちこくして・あかしんごう・を・むしした・ドライバー (driver who was late and disregarded [ran] a red light). This extended relative clause is contained in the sentence けいさつ・は・ちこくして・あかしんごう・を・むしした・ドライバー・を・とめました (the policeman stopped the driver who was late and disregarded [ran] a red light).[87]

Not only can one lengthen a relative clause, one can insert a relative clause within a relative clause. For example, the sentence かのじょ・は・じしん・が・ない・ひと・に・じょげん・を・あたえる・セラピストです (she is a therapist who gives advice to people who have no self-confidence) does just that. The

---

86   わたし I • かう to buy (う-verb) • きょうかしょ textbook • たかい expensive
87   けいさつ police • ちこくする to be late (する-verb) • あかしんごう red light • むしする to disregard (する-verb) • ドライバー driver • とめる to stop (る-verb)

relative clause じしん・が・ない・ひと (people who have no self confidence) is contained within the relative clause じしん・が・ない・ひと・に・じょげん・を・あたえる・セラピスト (therapist who gives advice to people who have no self-confidence).[88]

How does one read extended relative clauses with ease? It is recommended to analyze extended relative clauses by reading the words in reverse order. For example, consider how to analyze the extended relative clause じしん・が・ない・ひと・に・じょげん・を・あたえる・セラピスト (therapist who gives advice to people who have no self-confidence) by reading the words in reverse order. The last words of the relative clause are あたえる・セラピスト. Thus, the relative clause addresses a therapist who gives. The direct object particle を, which indicates what the therapist gives, marks the noun じょげん. Hence, the therapist gives advice. The indirect object particle に, which indicates who the therapist gives advice to, marks the noun ひと. Therefore, the therapist gives advice to people. The noun ひと is modified by the phrase じしん・が・ない. Accordingly, the therapist gives advice to people who have no self-confidence.

To create an extended relative clause that is grammatically correct, each modified noun must be immediately preceded by a verb, adjective, or noun in modifying form. (This chapter has explained what the modifying forms of words are.) To illustrate, consider how each modified noun in the sentence かのじょ・は・としょかん・で・はなす・ひと・に・まゆ・を・ひそめる・だいがくせいです (she is a college student who knits her brows [scowls] at people who talk in the library) is immediately preceded by a verb, adjective, or noun in modifying form. The sentence かのじょ・は・としょかん・で・はなす・ひと・に・まゆ・を・ひそめる・だいがくせいです contains two modified nouns. The first modified noun ひと, which is in the relative clause としょかん・で・はなす・ひと (people who talk in the library), is immediately preceded by the verb はなす. はなす is a modifying verb as informal basic verbs may modify nouns, and はなす employs the informal basic formula B3. While the first modified noun in the sentence is ひと, the second modified noun is だいがくせい, which is in the relative clause としょかん・で・はなす・ひと・に・まゆ・を・ひそ

---

[88] かのじょ she • じしん self confidence • ない nonexistent • ひと person • じょげん advice • あたえる to give (る-verb) • セラピスト therapist

める・だいがくせい (college student who knits her brows at people who talk in the library). だいがくせい is immediately preceded by the verb ひそめる. ひそめる is a modifying verb because informal basic verbs can modify nouns, and ひそめる employs the informal basic formula B3.[89]

---

[89] かのじょ she • としょかん library • はなす to speak (う-verb) • ひと person • まゆ eyebrow • ひそめる to knit (る-verb) • だいがくせい college student

NOMINALIZERS の AND こと

The nominalizers の and こと change phrases ending with a verb, い-adjective, or な-adjective into nouns. The verb, い-adjective, and な-adjective forms that modify nouns to create relative clauses modify the nominalizers の and こと. For example, informal basic verbs modify nominalizers since these forms modify nouns. Accordingly, たべない, which is the verb たべる conjugated according to the informal basic formula B1 + ない, modifies the nominalizer こと in the sentence やさい・を・たべない・こと・は・だめだ (not eating vegetables is bad). Likewise, ついた, which is the verb つく conjugated according to the informal basic formula Bた, modifies the nominalizer こと in the sentence かれ・が・わたし・に・うそ・を・ついた・こと・は・わたし・の・かんじょう・を・きずつけた (it hurt my feelings that he lied to me).[90]

As another example, informal obligation verbs modify nominalizers since these forms modify nouns. Consequently, しなければならない, which is the verb する conjugated according to the informal obligation formula B1 + なければならない, modifies the nominalizer の in the sentence あたらしい・じゅぎょういん・が・でんわ・の・トレーニング・を・しなければならない・の・は・かいしゃ・の・ほうしんです (it is company policy that new employees must do a phone training).[91]

90　やさい vegetable • たべる to eat (る-verb) • だめな no good • かれ he • わたし I • うそ lie • つく to tell (a lie) (う-verb) • かんじょう feelings • きずつける to hurt (る-verb)

91　あたらしい new • じゅぎょういん employee • でんわ phone • トレーニング training • する to do (irregular verb) • かいしゃ company • ほうしん policy

To provide yet another example, the dictionary form of な-adjectives modifies nouns and thus modifies nominalizers. That being the case, the dictionary form of the な-adjective けんこうな modifies the nominalizer こと in the sentence わたし・は・じぶん・が・けんこうな・こと・に・かんしゃしています (I am thankful that I am healthy).[92]

Other Function of の and こと

A phrase in which a verb, い-adjective, or な-adjective modifies の or こと can either be a nominalizer phrase, or a relative clause in which の or こと means "thing." For example, たべてはならない・の, in which the verb たべてはならない (must not eat) modifies の, can either be a nominalizer phrase meaning "having to not eat" or a relative clause meaning "thing that must not eat."[93]

Context indicates whether a phrase in which a verb, い-adjective, or な-adjective modifies の or こと is a nominalizer phrase or a relative clause in which の or こと means "thing." For example, context indicates that the phrase わたし・が・たべてはならない・の, in which the verb たべてはならない (must not eat) modifies の, is a relative clause in which の means "thing," in the sentence わたし・が・たべてはならない・の・は・ピーナツです (the thing that I must not eat is peanuts).

---

92 わたし I • じぶん myself • けんこうな healthy • かんしゃする to be grateful (する-verb)
93 わたし I • たべる to eat (る-verb) • ピーナツ peanut

APPENDIX A: PARTICLES

A noun particle assigns a noun a role in a sentence by immediately following the noun. For example, the noun particle で, which assigns a noun a role as a place of action, immediately follows the noun としょかん (library) to form the phrase としょかん・で (at the library).

While a noun particle assigns a noun a role, a compound sentence particle assigns an independent clause meaning in relation to a following independent clause. A compound sentence particle immediately follows the first independent clause. For example, the compound sentence particle から, which marks a reason, immediately follows the independent clause かのじょ・は・しょうじきです (she is honest) in the compound sentence かのじょ・は・しょうじきです・から、うそ・を・つきませんでした (she is honest, so she didn't tell a lie).[94]

Because an independent clause is a clause that would function as a sentence, not a fragment, without the other clauses of the sentence, a verb, い-adjective or copula that ends an independent clause is conjugated as if the verb, い-adjective or copula ended a sentence. For example, in the compound sentence かのじょ・は・しょうじきです・から、うそ・を・つきませんでした (she is honest, so she didn't tell a lie), the な-adjective しょうじきです, which ends an independent clause, is しょうじきな conjugated according to the sentence-ending formula stem + です.

---

94   かのじょ she • しょうじきな honest • うそ lie • つく to tell (a lie) (う-verb)

While a compound sentence particle assigns an independent clause meaning in relation to a following independent clause, a sentence particle alters the meaning or tone of a sentence. A sentence particle is inserted at the end of a sentence. For example, the sentence particle よ, which expresses emphasis, may be inserted at the end of the sentence あなた・は・ちがいます (you are wrong) to form あなた・は・ちがいます・よ (you are wrong!).[95]

There are also anomalous particles. Unlike sentence particles, compound sentence particles, and noun particles, each anomalous particle assigns meaning to a different type of sentence component. See the description of each anomalous particle for information regarding each particle's usage.

Particle Chart

Abbreviation	Particle Type
N	Noun Particle
C	Compound Sentence Particle
S	Sentence Particle
A	Anomalous Particle

Particle	Type	Function	English Equivalent
は (wa)	N	Marks a topic	as for
Example:		わたし・は・いやです。[96] As for me, it is unpleasant.	
が (ga)	N	Marks a subject	NA
		わたし・は・ジョギング・が・すきです。[97] I like jogging.	
が (ga)	C	Expresses contradiction	but
Example:		わたし・は・じぶん・に・メモ・を・かきましたが、わすれました。[98] I wrote myself a note, but I forgot.	

---

95 あなた you • ちがう to be wrong (う-verb)
96 わたし I • いやな unpleasant
97 わたし I • ジョギング jogging • すきな like
98 わたし I • じぶん myself • メモ note • かく to write (う-verb) • わすれる to forget (る-verb)

Particle	Type	Function	English Equivalent
が (ga)	C	Functions as a softener	NA
Example:		すみません・が、トイレ・は・どこです・か。[99] Excuse me, where is the restroom?	
を (o)	N	Marks a direct object	NA
Example:		わたし・は・さら・を・あらいました。[100] I washed the dishes.	
を (o)	N	Marks a place a noun leaves from or passes through	from; through
Example:		かのじょ・は・へや・を・でました。[101] She left the room.	
で (de)	N	Marks a place of action	at
Example:		わたし・は・レストラン・で・たべました。[102] I ate at a restaurant.	
で (de)	N	Marks an implement of an action	by means of
Example:		わたし・は・でんしゃ・で・りょこうしました。[103] I travelled by means of a train.	
に (ni)	N	Marks a place of existence	at; in
Example:		かいぎ・に・じょうし・が・います。[104] The boss is at a meeting.	
に (ni)	N	Marks a time	at; on
Example:		かのじょ・は・にちようび・に・きょうかい・に・いきます。[105] On Sunday she goes to church.	
に (ni)	N	Marks a place of destination	to
Example:		わたし・は・コンビニ・に・いきます。[106] I will go to the convenience store.	

---

99 すみません excuse me • トイレ restroom • どこ where

100 わたし I • さら dish • あらう to wash (う-verb)

101 かのじょ she • へや room • でる to exit (る-verb)

102 わたし I • レストラン restaurant • たべる to eat (る-verb)

103 わたし I • でんしゃ train • りょこうする to travel (する-verb)

104 かいぎ meeting • じょうし boss • いる to exist (る-verb)

105 かのじょ she • にちようび Sunday • きょうかい church • いく to go (う-verb)

106 わたし I • コンビニ convenience store • いく to go (う-verb)

Particle	Type	Function	English Equivalent
に (ni)	N	Marks an indirect object	to
Example:		わたし・は・ともだち・に・はなしました。[107] I spoke to my friend.	
に (ni)	A	Marks a purpose	for; to
Example:		わたし・は・うんどう・を・し・に・ジム・に・いきます。[108] I will go to the gym to exercise.	
に (ni)	N	Marks a noun of a list	and
Example:		わたし・の・かけい・は・スコットランドじん・に・アイルランドじん・に・イギリスじんです。[109] My ancestry is Scottish, Irish, and English.	
へ (e)	N	Marks a place of direction	to; towards
Example:		わたし・は・ちかてつ・の・えき・へ・あるきます。[110] I will walk to/towards the subway station.	
から (kara)	N	Marks an origin	from
Example:		わたし・は・ひので・から・のうじょう・で・はたらきます。[111] I work on the farm from sunrise.	
から (kara)	C	Marks a reason	so
Example:		わたし・は・しょくりょう・が・いります・から、スーパー・に・いきます。[112] I need groceries, so I will go to the supermarket.	
まで (made)	N	Marks a terminus	until; to
Example:		まつり・は・よる・まで・つづきます。[113] The festival will continue until night.	
の (no)	N	Marks a modifying noun	NA
Example:		それ・は・しょうねん・の・かばんです。[114] That is the boy's bag.	

---

[107] わたし I • ともだち friend • はなす to speak (う-verb)

[108] わたし I • うんどう exercise • する to do (irregular verb) • ジム gym • いく to go (う-verb)

[109] わたし I • かけい family lineage • スコットランドじん Scottish person • アイルランドじん Irish person • イギリスじん British person

[110] わたし I • ちかてつ subway • えき station • あるく to walk (う-verb)

[111] わたし I • ひので sunrise • のうじょう agricultural farm • はたらく to work (う-verb)

[112] わたし I • しょくりょう food • いる to need (う-verb) • スーパー supermarket • いく to go (う-verb)

[113] まつり festival • よる night • つづく to continue (う-verb)

[114] それ that • しょうねん boy • かばん bag

Particle	Type	Function	English Equivalent
の (no)	S	Functions as an informal verbal question mark	?
Example:		かれ・は・どこ・に・いった・の。[115] Where did he go?	
の (no)	S	Functions as a softener	NA
Example:		わたし・は・しらない・の。[116] I don't know.	
と (to)	N	Marks a noun of a list	and
Example:		わたし・の・かけい・は・スコットランドじん・と・アイルランドじん・と・イギリスじんです。[117] My ancestry is Scottish, Irish, and English.	
と (to)	A	Marks dialogue or thoughts	NA
Example:		わたし・は・おもしろかった・と・おもいました。[118] I thought it was interesting.	
と (to)	N	Marks an accompanying noun	with
Example:		わたし・は・ホストファミリー・と・にほんご・を・れんしゅうします。[119] I will practice Japanese with my host family.	
と (to)	A	Expresses a condition	if
Example:		まっすぐ・いく・と、もくてきち・に・とうちゃくします。[120] If you go straight, you will arrive at the destination.	
や (ya)	N	Marks a noun of an incomplete list	and
Example:		わたし・の・さいふ・の・なか・に・うんてんめんきょしょう・や・デビットカード・や・クレジットカード・が・ありました。[121] Inside my wallet were a driver's license, debit card, and credit card (in addition to other items).	

---

[115] かれ he • どこ where • いく to go (う-verb)

[116] わたし I • しる to know (う-verb)

[117] わたし I • かけい family lineage • スコットランドじん Scottish person • アイルランドじん Irish person • イギリスじん British person

[118] わたし I • おもしろい interesting • おもう to think (う-verb)

[119] わたし I • ホストファミリー host family • にほんご Japanese • れんしゅうする to practice (する-verb)

[120] まっすぐ straight • いく to go (う-verb) • もくてきち destination • とうちゃくする to arrive (する-verb)

[121] わたし I • さいふ wallet • なか inside • うんてんめんきょしょう driver's license • デビットカード debit card • クレジットカード credit card • ある to exist (う-verb)

Particle	Type	Function	English Equivalent
も (mo)	N	Marks an additional noun	too; also; both
Example:		わたし・は・その・かいが・も・かいます。[122] I will buy that painting too.	
も (mo)	N	Marks a quantity	as much as; as many as; not even
Example:		わたし・は・クッキー・を・２０(にじゅう)・まい・も・たべました。[123] I ate as many as 20 cookies.	
か (ka)	S	Functions as a verbal question mark	?
Example:		あなた・は・どうして・それ・を・しました・か。[124] Why did you do that?	
か (ka)	N	Marks an option of a list	or
Example:		コメディ・か・スリラー・を・みたいです・か。[125] Do you want to watch a comedy or thriller?	
ね (ne)	S	Functions as an agreement seeker	isn't it?
Example:		てんき・は・すばらしいです・ね。[126] The weather is splendid, isn't it?	
よ (yo)	S	Expresses emphasis	!
Example:		わたし・は・はんたいします・よ。[127] I disagree!	

Topic Particle は and Subject Particle が

There are a number of differences between topic particle は (pronounced as "wa" although the hiragana は is normally pronounced as "ha") and subject particle が. One of these differences is that a noun in the modifying phrase of a relative clause can be marked with subject particle が but cannot be marked

---

[122] わたし I • その that • かいが painting • かう to buy (う-verb)

[123] わたし I • クッキー cookie • にじゅう 20 • まい (counter for cookies) • たべる to eat (る-verb)

[124] あなた you • どうして why • それ that • する to do (irregular verb)

[125] コメディ comedy • スリラー thriller • みる to see (る-verb)

[126] てんき weather • すばらしい splendid

[127] わたし I • はんたいする to object (する-verb)

with topic particle は. For example, わたし (I) is marked with subject particle が in the modifying phrase わたし・が・きのう・みた (that I saw yesterday) of the relative clause わたし・が・きのう・みた・えいが (the movie that I saw yesterday). The relative clause わたし・は・きのう・みた・えいが (the movie that I saw yesterday), in which わたし is marked with topic particle は, is grammatically incorrect.

Although a noun in the modifying phrase of a relative clause cannot be marked with topic particle は, the modified noun of a relative clause can be marked with topic particle は. For example, in the sentence わたし・が・きのう・みた・えいが・は・ながいです (the movie that I saw yesterday is long), the modified noun えいが (movie) of the relative clause わたし・が・きのう・みた・えいが (the movie that I saw yesterday) is marked with the topic particle は.[128]

Similarly to how a noun in the modifying phrase of a relative clause cannot be marked with topic particle は but the modified noun of a relative clause can be marked with topic particle は, a noun in the modifying phrase of a nominalizer phrase cannot be marked with topic particle は but a nominalizer can be marked with topic particle は. For example, the noun ひんこん (poverty) is marked with subject particle が instead of topic particle は in the modifying phrase グローバルな・ひんこん・が・へっている (global poverty is lessening) of the nominalizer phrase グローバルな・ひんこん・が・へっている・の. Unlike ひんこん, the nominalizer の is marked with topic particle は in the sentence グローバルな・ひんこん・が・へっている・の・は・いい・ことです (it is a good thing that global poverty is lessening).[129]

Not only does the usage of topic particle は and subject particle が differ with a nominalizer phrase, the usage of topic particle は and subject particle が usually differ when an independent clause contains one noun marked with topic particle は and one noun marked with subject particle が. When an independent clause contains one noun marked with topic particle は and one noun marked with subject particle が, usually the main topic of the independent clause is marked with topic particle は, while the subtopic of the

---

128 わたし I • きのう yesterday • みる to see (る-verb) • えいが movie • ながい long

129 グローバルな global • ひんこん poverty • へる to decrease (う-verb) • いい good • こと thing

independent clause is marked with subject particle が. To illustrate, the main topic わたし (I) of the independent clause わたし・は・チョコレート・が・すきです (I like chocolate) is marked with topic particle は. チョコレート is the subtopic of the main topic わたし because chocolate addresses the person's preferences. As the subtopic, チョコレート is the marked with subject particle が.[130]

Another example of an independent clause in which the main topic is marked with topic particle は while the subtopic is marked with subject particle が is ぞう・は・みみ・が・おおきいです (as for elephants, their ears are large). The main topic ぞう (elephants) is marked with topic particle は. みみ is the subtopic of the main topic ぞう since ears address the elephant body. The subtopic みみ is marked with subject particle が.[131]

Also consider how the main topic is marked with topic particle は whereas the subtopic is marked with subject particle が in the independent clause わたし・は・ペット・が・ほしいです (I want a pet). The main topic わたし (I) is marked with topic particle は. ペット is the subtopic of the main topic わたし because a pet addresses the person's wish. As the subtopic, ペット is marked with subject particle が.[132]

What is the function of topic particle は in sentences that end with a causative verb? Because a causative verb means "to make/let do the verb," the topic of a causative verb is the noun that makes or lets an indirect object do the verb. For example, the topic けいさつ (police officer) makes the indirect object ドライバー (driver) do the verb (exit) in the sentence けいさつ・は・ドライバー・に・くるま・を・おりさせました (the police officer made the driver exit the car).[133]

Whereas the topic of a causative verb makes or lets an indirect object do the verb, the topic of a passive verb has a different function. Because a passive verb means "to have the verb done to one," the topic of a passive verb is the noun that the verb is done to. For example, the verb (spreading) is done to the topic びょうき (disease) in the sentence びょうき・は・か・に・ひろめられます (the disease is spread by mosquitoes).[134]

---

130 わたし I • チョコレート chocolate • すきな like
131 ぞう elephant • みみ ear • おおきい large
132 わたし I • ペット pet • ほしい want
133 けいさつ police • ドライバー driver • くるま car • おりる to get out of (る-verb)
134 びょうき disease • か mosquito • ひろめる to spread (る-verb)

While the topic of a passive verb has the verb done to it, the topic of a causative passive verb has a different function. Because a causative passive verb means "to be made to do the verb," the topic of a causative passive verb is the noun that is made to do the verb. For example, the topic こども (child) is made to do the verb (do) in the sentence こども・は・りょうしん・に・しゅくだい・を・させられます (the child is made to do their homework by the parent).[135]

Although topic particle は and subject particle が possess different functions in some instances, in other instances topic particle は and subject particle が are interchangeable. That is to say, marking a noun with は instead of が, or vice versa, sometimes produces an identical or very similar sentence meaning. For example, both かれ・は・やくしゃです, in which かれ is marked with は, and かれ・が・やくしゃです, in which かれ is marked with が, mean "he is an actor."[136]

Because the usage of topic particle は and subject particle が is one of the most complex aspects of Japanese grammar, and a comprehensive explanation would be exceedingly long, only a brief introduction to topic particle は and subject particle が is provided in this book.

Direct Object Particle を, Transitive Verbs, and Intransitive Verbs

Transitive verbs are verbs that can take direct objects. A direct object is a noun that a subject/topic does a transitive verb to. To illustrate, the topic じゅうぎょういん (employee) does the transitive verb いれる (put in) to the direct object ふくろ (bag) in the sentence じゅうぎょういん・は・ふくろ・に・レシート・を・いれる (the employee puts the receipt in the bag). As another example, the topic わたし (I) does the transitive verb あける (open) to the direct object ドア (door) in the sentence わたし・は・ドア・を・あける (I will open the door).[137]

---

135 こども child • りょうしん parents • しゅくだい homework • する to do (irregular verb)
136 かれ he • やくしゃ actor
137 じゅうぎょういん employee • ふくろ bag • レシート receipt • いれる to put in (る-verb) • わたし I • ドア door • あける to open (る-verb)

A direct object is normally marked with direct object particle を. For example, the direct object レシート (receipt) is marked with direct object particle を in the sentence じゅうぎょういん・は・ふくろ・に・レシート・を・いれる (the employee puts the receipt in the bag). Likewise, the direct object ドア (door) is marked with direct object particle を in the sentence わたし・は・ドア・を・あける (I will open the door).

Although a direct object is normally marked with direct object particle を, the direct object of a potential verb is marked with subject particle が. For example, the direct object オペラ (opera) of the potential verb うたえる (to be able to sing) is marked with subject particle が in the sentence かのじょ・は・オペラ・が・うたえます (she can sing opera). The sentence かのじょ・は・オペラ・を・うたえます, in which the direct object オペラ is marked with direct object particle を, is grammatically incorrect.[138]

Whereas transitive verbs can take direct objects, intransitive verbs cannot take direct objects. In other words, while a noun does a transitive verb to a direct object, a noun does an intransitive verb with no direct object involved. To illustrate, consider how a noun does the intransitive verb はじまる (to begin) with no direct object involved. In the sentence ぎきょく・が・はじまりました (the play began), the subject ぎきょく (play) does the intransitive verb はじまる (begins). As another example, consider how a noun does the intransitive verb あく (to open) with no direct object involved. In the sentence ドア・が・あく (the door opens), the subject ドア (door) does the intransitive verb あく (opens).[139]

Indirect Object Particle に

In sentences that do not end with a causative, passive, or causative passive verb, the indirect object is the noun that is the recipient of the verb. For example, the indirect object クラスメート (classmates) is the recipient of the verb (reading) in the sentence がくせい・は・クラスメート・に・ほん・を・よみました (the student read the book to the classmates).[140]

---

138 かのじょ she • オペラ opera • うたう to sing (う-verb)
139 ぎきょく play • はじまる to begin (う-verb) • ドア door • あく to open (う-verb)
140 がくせい student • クラスメート classmate • ほん book • よむ to read (う-verb)

Although the indirect object of a sentence that does not end with a causative, passive, or causative passive verb is the recipient of the verb, an indirect object has a different function in a sentence ending with a passive verb. The function of the indirect object of a passive verb is determined by the function of the topic. Because a passive verb means "to have the verb done to one," the topic of a passive verb is the noun that the verb is done to. As the topic is the noun that the verb is done to, the indirect object is the noun that does the verb to the topic. For example, the indirect object いぬ (dog) does the verb (eats) to the topic (cake) in the sentence ケーキ・は・いぬ・に・たべられました (the cake was eaten by the dog).[141]

Whereas the indirect object of a passive verb does the verb to the topic, the indirect object of a causative verb has a different function. The function of the topic of a causative verb determines the function of the indirect object. Since a causative verb means "to make/let do the verb," the topic of a causative verb is the noun that makes or lets an indirect object do the verb. Because the topic is the noun that makes or lets an indirect object do the verb, the indirect object is the noun that is made or allowed to do the verb. To demonstrate, the indirect object がくせい (students) is made to do the verb (read) by the topic (teacher) in the sentence せんせい・は・がくせい・に・ほん・を・よませました (the teacher made the students read the book).[142]

While the indirect object of a causative verb is made or allowed to do the verb, the indirect object of a causative passive verb does something else. The function of the indirect object of a causative passive verb is determined by the function of the topic. Because a causative passive verb means "to be made to do the verb," the topic of a causative passive verb is the noun that is made to do the verb. As the topic is the noun that is made to do the verb, the indirect object is the noun that makes the topic do the verb. For example, the indirect object けいさつ (police) makes the topic (person) do the verb (raise) in the sentence ひと・は・けいさつ・に・て・を・あげさせられました (the person was made to raise their hands by the police).[143]

---

141 ケーキ cake • いぬ dog • たべる to eat (る-verb)
142 せんせい teacher • がくせい student • ほん book • よむ to read (う-verb)
143 ひと person • けいさつ policeman • て hand • あげる to raise (る-verb)

Purpose Particle に

Purpose particle に follows B2. (B2 refers to verb base two. For information regarding verb bases, see the verb base section of this book.) B2 + purpose particle に means "to do the verb." For example, おどり・に, which contains purpose particle に and the B2 おどり of おどる, means "to dance." As おどり・に means "to dance," the sentence わたし・は・おどり・に・バー・に・いきます means "I will go to the bar to dance."[144]

Direction Particle へ

Although the hiragana へ is normally pronounced as "he," direction particle へ is pronounced as "e."

Modifying Particle の

Modifying particle の is inserted between a modifying noun and a modified noun. The modifying noun precedes の, while the modified noun follows の. For example, the modifying noun おとこ (male) precedes の while the modified noun ひと (person) follows の in the phrase おとこ・の・ひと (male person).[145]

When the modifying noun that precedes の is an identity, and the modified noun that follows の is a possessed noun, の creates a possessive phrase. For example, in the possessive phrase はなよめ・の・ゆびわ (bride's ring), the modifying noun that precedes の is the identity はなよめ (bride), and the modified noun that follows の is the possessed noun ゆびわ (ring).[146]

In some instances, the modifying noun that precedes の is the equivalent of an adjective, not a noun, in English. That is to say, some Japanese nouns translate as English adjectives. For example, ふつう (regular) is a Japanese

---

144 わたし I • おどる to dance (う-verb) • バー bar • いく to go (う-verb)
145 おとこ male • ひと person
146 はなよめ bride • ゆびわ ring

noun although "regular" is an English adjective. Accordingly, ふつう can precede の as a modifying noun in the phrase ふつう・の・てんき (regular weather).[147]

Similarly to how some Japanese nouns translate as English adjectives, some Japanese nouns translate as English prepositions or prepositional phrases. For example, in the phrase ゆうびんきょく・の・まえ (before the post office; in front of the post office), まえ is a Japanese noun but translates as the preposition "before" or the prepositional phrase "in front of."[148]

Verbal Question Mark Particles か and の

In modern Japanese, the informal verbal question mark particle の ends informal sentences but does not end formal sentences. For example, informal verbal question mark particle の ends the informal sentence あなた・は・なに・を・する・の (what will you do?). This sentence is informal because the verb する employs the informal formula B3. On the other hand, the sentence あなた・は・なに・を・します・の would not be used because します is the verb する conjugated according to the formal formula B2 + ます.[149]

Although informal verbal question mark particle の only ends informal sentences in modern Japanese, verbal question mark particle か ends both informal and formal sentences. For example, verbal question mark particle か ends the informal sentence いつ・はじまる・か (when does it start?). This sentence is informal because はじまる employs the informal formula B3. Additionally, verbal question mark particle か ends the formal sentence いつ・はじまります・か (when does it start?). This sentence is formal because はじまります is the verb はじまる conjugated according to the formal formula B2 + ます.[150]

While verbalizing a question, a verbal question mark particle may be stated but is not required. When a verbal question mark particle is not stated, a rising intonation is commonly used to indicate that a sentence is a question.

---

147 ふつう regular • てんき weather
148 ゆうびんきょく post office • まえ in front of
149 あなた you • なに what • する to do (irregular verb)
150 いつ when • はじまる to start (う-verb)

Softener Particle の

The informal softener particle の usually ends informal sentences. For example, informal softener particle の ends the informal sentence わたし・は・み ず・が・いる・の (I need water). This sentence is informal because the verb いる employs the informal formula B3.[151]

Sometimes softener particle の is used in formal situations, such as by shop staff. For example, softener particle の is used in the sentence きょう・は・ みせ・が・あいていないです・の (the shop is closed today).[152]

Dialogue and Thoughts Particle と

Dialogue/thoughts particle と follows dialogue quotes and thought quotes. For example, dialogue/thoughts particle と follows the dialogue quote しょく じ・が・おいしかった (the meal was delicious) in the sentence かのじょ・は・し ょくじ・が・おいしかった・と・いいました (she said the meal was delicious).[153]

Direct dialogue quotes and direct thought quotes are surrounded with Japanese quotation marks (「」). For instance, the direct dialogue quote 「あ かちゃん・は・ねている」 ("the baby is sleeping") is surrounded with Japanese quotation marks in the sentence かのじょ・は・「あかちゃん・は・ねている」と・ ささやきました (she whispered "the baby is sleeping").[154]

Whereas direct dialogue quotes and direct thought quotes are surrounded with Japanese quotation marks, indirect dialogue quotes and indirect thought quotes are not surrounded with Japanese quotation marks. For example, the indirect dialogue quote あかちゃん・が・ねている (the baby is sleeping) in the sentence かのじょ・は・あかちゃん・が・ねている・と・ささやきました (she whispered that the baby is sleeping) is not surrounded with Japanese quotation marks.

---

151 わたし I • みず water • いる to need (う-verb)
152 きょう today • みせ store • あく to open (う-verb)
153 かのじょ she • しょくじ meal • おいしい delicious • いう to say (う-verb)
154 かのじょ she • あかちゃん baby • ねる to sleep (る-verb) •
ささやく to whisper (う-verb)

Indirect dialogue quotes and indirect thought quotes, which are not surrounded with Japanese quotation marks, are informal. For example, the indirect dialogue quote しけん・が・むずかしかった (the test was difficult) is informal in the sentence かのじょ・は・しけん・が・むずかしかった・と・いいました (she said the test was difficult) as むずかしかった is the い-adjective むずかしい conjugated according to the informal formula stem + かった.[155]

Like indirect dialogue quotes and indirect thought quotes, direct thought quotes are informal. Direct thought quotes are informal because direct thought quotes directly quote thoughts and people think in informal language. For example, the direct thought quote うそだろう (it is probably a lie) in the sentence かれ・は「うそだろう」・と・おもいました (he thought "it is probably a lie") is informal. We can see that うそだろう is informal because だろう is an informal copula.[156]

While direct thought quotes are always informal, some direct dialogue quotes are informal whereas other direct dialogue quotes are formal. Because direct dialogue quotes directly reflect what was said, a direct dialogue quote is informal if the quoted dialogue is informal. Likewise, if the quoted dialogue is formal, a direct dialogue quote is formal. To demonstrate how some direct dialogue quotes are informal while other direct dialogue quotes are formal, consider the following examples. The direct dialogue quote 「わたしたち・の・デート・は・たのしかった」 ("our date was fun") in the sentence かれ・は「わたしたち・の・デート・は・たのしかった」・と・いいました (he said "our date was fun") is informal. It is evident that the direct dialogue quote 「わたしたち・の・デート・は・たのしかった」 is informal because たのしかった is the い-adjective たのしい conjugated according to the informal formula stem + かった. In contrast, the direct dialogue quote 「しつもん・が・あります」 ("I have a question") in the sentence かれ・は「しつもん・が・あります」・と・いいました (he said "I have a question") is formal. We can see that the direct dialogue quote 「しつもん・が・あります」 is formal because あります is the verb ある conjugated according to the formal formula B2 + ます.[157]

---

[155] かのじょ she • しけん test • むずかしい difficult • いう to say (う-verb)
[156] かれ he • うそ lie • おもう to think (う-verb)
[157] かれ he • わたしたち we • デート date • たのしい fun • いう to say (う-verb) • しつもん question • ある to have (う-verb)

Conditional Particle と

Conditional particle と follows the informal basic non-past forms of verbs, adjectives and copulas. For example, conditional particle と follows べんきょうしない, which is the verb べんきょうする conjugated according to the informal basic non-past formula B1 + ない, in the sentence あなた・が・べんきょうしない・と、テスト・は・むずかしいです (if you don't study, the test will be difficult). Likewise, conditional particle と follows the い-adjective はやい, which employs the informal basic non-past formula dict., in the sentence ジェットコースター・が・はやい・と、わたし・は・はきます (if the roller coaster is fast, I will vomit). As another example, in the sentence アパート・が・きれいでない・と、わたし・は・そうじします (if the apartment is not neat, I will clean) conditional particle と follows きれいでない, which is the な-adjective きれいな conjugated according to the informal basic non-past formula stem + でない. By the same token, conditional particle と follows はれだ, which contains the noun はれ and the informal basic non-past copula だ, in the sentence てんき・が・はれだ・と、わたし・は・そと・で・ちゅうしょく・を・たべます (if the weather is sunny, I will eat lunch outside).[158]

Although informal basic *past* verbs, adjectives, and copulas cannot precede conditional particle と, informal basic non-past verbs, adjectives, and copulas preceding conditional particle と may have a past tense meaning. When a verb, adjective, or copula preceding と has a past tense meaning, said verb, adjective, or copula is non-conditional. For example, although はなしている is conjugated according to the progressive informal basic *non-past* formula Bて + いる, はなしている・と translates as the past tense non-conditional phrase "when was talking" in the sentence かれ・と・はなしている・と、でんわ・が・なりました (when I was talking with him, the phone rang).[159]

---

158 あなた you • べんきょうする to study (する-verb) • テスト test • むずかしい difficult • ジェットコースター roller coaster • はやい fast • わたし I • はく to vomit (う-verb) • アパート apartment • きれいな neat • そうじする to clean (する-verb) • てんき weather • はれ sunny weather • そと outside • ちゅうしょく lunch • たべる to eat (る-verb)

159 かれ he • はなす to talk (う-verb) • でんわ telephone • なる to ring (う-verb)

A sentence employing conditional particle と may be informal or formal depending on the formality level of the sentence-ending verb, い-adjective, or copula. For example, the sentence わたし・は・うんどうする・と、きんにく・が・つきます (if I exercise, I will gain muscle) is formal because the sentence-ending verb つきます is the verb つく (to gain [muscle]) conjugated according to the formal formula B2 + ます. Likewise, the sentence へや・が・くらい・と、わたし・は・でんき・を・つける (if the room is dark, I will turn on a light) is informal because the sentence-ending verb つける (to turn on) employs the informal formula B3.[160]

Additional Noun Particle も

When additional noun particle も marks one noun, additional noun particle も translates as "too" or "also." For example, additional noun particle も translates as "too" or "also" in the sentence かのじょ・も・その・ほん・を・よみました (she too read that book; she also read that book).[161]

When additional noun particle も marks two or more nouns, additional noun particle も creates a list meaning "both nouns." For example, additional noun particle も creates a list meaning "both she and he" in the sentence かのじょ・も・かれ・も・わらいました (both she and he laughed).[162]

Quantity Particle も

Quantity particle も means "as much as/as many as" in phrases with an affirmative meaning, and means "not even" in phrases with a negative meaning. For example, quantity particle も means "as much as" in the affirmative sentence しょくじ・は・１００００(いちまん)・えん・も・かかる (the meal costs as much as

---

160 わたし I • うんどうする to exercise (する-verb) • きんにく muscle •
つく to gain (muscle) (う-verb) • へや room • くらい dark • でんき light •
つける to turn on (る-verb)
161 かのじょ she • その that • ほん book • よむ to read (う-verb)
162 かのじょ she • かれ he • わらう to laugh (う-verb)

10,000 yen). This sentence has an affirmative meaning because the verb かかる employs the affirmative formula B3. In contrast, quantity particle も means "not even" in the negative sentence パーティー・に・１０(じゅう)・にん・も・きませんでした (not even 10 people came to the party). This sentence has a negative meaning because きませんでした is the verb くる conjugated according to the negative formula B2 + ませんでした.[163]

---

[163] しょくじ meal • いちまん 100,000 • えん yen • かかる to cost (う-verb) • パーティー party • じゅう 10 • にん (counter for people) • くる to come (irregular verb)

APPENDIX B: SENTENCE STRUCTURES

The sentence structures listed in this appendix contain standard word order. For example, the sentence structure "Topic + は + Indirect Object + に + Direct Object + を + Action Verb" (meaning "the topic does the action to the direct object to the indirect object") contains standard word order. That is to say, normally the topic precedes the indirect object, the indirect object precedes the direct object, and the direct object precedes the action verb. A sentence containing this standard sentence structure is かのじょ・は・せきじゅうじ・に・１０，０００(いちまん)・ドル・を・きふした, which means "she donated $10,000 to the Red Cross."[164]

Although the sentence structures listed in this appendix contain standard word order, the placement of the nouns within the sentence structures is flexible. If more emphasis on a noun is desired, the noun and its corresponding particle are moved closer to the beginning of the sentence. For example, suppose more emphasis on the noun せきじゅうじ (Red Cross) was desired in the sentence かのじょ・は・せきじゅうじ・に・１０，０００(いちまん)・ドル・を・きふした (she donated $10,000 to the Red Cross). To put it another way, suppose one wished to emphasize how the woman donated to the Red Cross instead of other organizations. To place more emphasis on the noun せきじゅ

---

[164] かのじょ she • せきじゅうじ Red Cross • いちまん 10,000 • ドル dollar • きふする to donate (する-verb)

うじ, the noun せきじゅうじ and its corresponding particle に can be placed before かのじょ and its corresponding particle は. In the sentence せきじゅうじ・に・かのじょ・は・１００００(いちまん)・ドル・を・きふした，せきじゅうじ・に is placed before かのじょ・は.

Topic + は + Subject + が〜
As for the topic, the subject~
わたし・は・びじゅつかん・が・すきです。[165] I like art museums. (As for myself, like art museums.)

Ｂて + も + Permissive Word
The action is allowed.
すわって・も・いいです・よ。[166] You may sit down.

Ｂて + は + Prohibitive Word
The action is prohibited.
わたし・の・にっき・を・よんで・は・だめです。[167] You may not read my diary.

Topic/Subject + は/が + Origin + から〜
The topic/subject from the origin~
かみ・は・き・から・つくられます。[168] Paper is made from trees.

Topic/Subject + は/が + Terminus + まで〜
The topic/subject until the terminus~
わたし・は・ひる・まで・テニス・の・れんしゅう・を・します。[169] I will practice tennis until noon.

---

[165] わたし I • びじゅつかん art museum • すきな like
[166] すわる to sit (う-verb) • いい good
[167] わたし I • にっき diary • よむ to read (う-verb) • だめな no good
[168] かみ paper • き tree • つくる to make (う-verb)
[169] わたし I • ひる noon • テニス tennis • れんしゅう practice • する to do (irregular verb)

Topic/Subject + は/が + Origin + から + Terminus + まで~
The topic/subject from the origin until the terminus~
わたし・は・きょうと・から・とうきょう・まで・りょこうします。[170] I will travel from Kyoto to Tokyo.

Topic/Subject + は/が + Place of Existence + に + Existence Verb
The topic/subject exists at the place of existence.
わたし・は・コンサート・に・います。 I will be at a concert.

Topic/Subject + は/が + Time + に + Place of Existence + に + Existence Verb
At the time, the topic/subject exists at the place of existence.
わたし・は・7(しち)・がつ・18(じゅうはち)・にち・に・コンサート・に・います。[171] On July 18th, I will be at a concert.

Topic/Subject + は/が + Place of Destination + に or へ + Direction Verb
The topic/subject goes to the place of destination.
わたし・は・としょかん・に・いきます。 I will go to the library.

Topic/Subject + は/が + Implement of the Action + で + Place of Destination + に or へ + Direction Verb
The topic/subject goes to the place of destination by means of the implement of the action.
わたし・は・バス・で・としょかん・に・いきます。 I will go to the library by bus.

---

170 わたし I・きょうと Kyoto・とうきょう Tokyo・りょこうする to travel (する-verb)

171 わたし I・しち 7・がつ month・じゅうはち 18・にち day of the month・コンサート concert・いる to be (る-verb)

Topic/Subject + は/が + Time + に + Implement of the Action + で + Place of Destination + に or へ + Direction Verb
At the time, the topic/subject goes to the place of destination by means of the implement of the action.
わたし・は・げつようび・に・バス・で・としょかん・に・いきます。[172]   On Monday, I will go to the library by bus.

Topic/Subject + は/が + Direct Object + を + Action Verb
The topic/subject does the action to the direct object.
わたし・は・イベント・を・せんでんしました。 I advertised the event.

Topic/Subject + は/が + Indirect Object + に + Direct Object + を + Action Verb
The topic/subject does the action to the direct object to the indirect object.
わたし・は・わかもの・に・イベント・を・せんでんしました。 I advertised the event to young people.

Topic/Subject + は/が + Implement of the Action + で + Indirect Object + に + Direct Object + を + Action Verb
The topic/subject does the action to the direct object to the indirect object by means of the implement of the action.
わたし・は・オンライン・こうこく・で・わかもの・に・イベント・を・せんでんしました。 I advertised the event to young people by means of online ads.

Topic/Subject + は/が + Place of Action + で + Implement of the Action + で + Indirect Object + に + Direct Object + を + Action Verb
At the place of action, the topic/subject does the action to the direct object to the indirect object by means of the implement of the action.
わたし・は・ニューヨークし・で・オンライン・こうこく・で・わかもの・に・イベント・を・せんでんしました。 In New York City, I advertised the event to young people by means of online ads.

---

[172] わたし I • げつようび Monday • バス bus • としょかん library • いく to go (う-verb)

Topic/Subject + は/が + Time + に + Place of Action + で + Implement of the Action + で + Indirect Object + に + Direct Object + を + Action Verb
At the time at the place of action, the topic/subject does the action to the direct object to the indirect object by means of the implement of the action.
わたし・は・なつ・に・ニューヨークし・で・オンライン・こうこく・で・わかもの・に・イベント・を・せんでんしました。[173] In summer in New York City, I advertised the event to young people by means of online ads.

---

[173] わたし I • なつ summer • ニューヨークし New York City • オンライン online • こうこく ad • わかもの young people • イベント event • せんでんする to advertise (する-verb)

APPENDIX C: DICTIONARY

い-adjectives, な-adjectives, and verbs are provided in dictionary form.

A			
Reading	Word	Translation	Word Type
abiru	あびる	to take (a shower)	transitive る-verb
agaru	あがる	to rise	intransitive う-verb
ageru	あげる	to raise	transitive る-verb
airurandojin	アイルランドじん	Irish person	noun
aitemu	アイテム	item	noun
akachan	あかちゃん	baby	noun
akashingou	あかしんごう	red traffic light	noun
akeru	あける	to open	transitive る-verb
akirameru	あきらめる	to give up	transitive る-verb
aku	あく	to open	intransitive う-verb
amai	あまい	sweet (taste)	い-adjective
amari	あまり	not much	adverb
ame	あめ	rain	noun
anata	あなた	you	noun

A

Reading	Word	Translation	Word Type
antiiku	アンティーク	antique	noun
apaato	アパート	apartment	noun
arau	あらう	to wash	transitive う-verb
are	あれ	that (referring to a noun distance from both the speaker and listener)	noun
aru	ある	to be; to exist; to have	intransitive う-verb
aruku	あるく	to walk	transitive う-verb
ashita	あした	tomorrow	noun
ataeru	あたえる	to give	transitive る-verb
atarashii	あたらしい	new	い-adjective
atsui	あつい	hot; thick	い-adjective
au	あう	to meet	intransitive う-verb

B

Reading	Word	Translation	Word Type
baa	バー	bar	noun
baai	ばあい	case; situation	noun
bando	バンド	band	noun
bara	バラ	rose	noun
basu	バス	bus	noun
bengoshi	べんごし	lawyer	noun
benkyousuru	べんきょうする	to study	transitive する-verb
bijutsukan	びじゅつかん	art museum	noun
bukka	ぶっか	cost of living	noun
buuke	ブーケ	bouquet	noun
byouki	びょうき	sickness; disease	noun
byoukina	びょうきな	sick	な-adjective

C

Reading	Word	Translation	Word Type
chigau	ちがう	to be wrong	intransitive う-verb
chikai	ちかい	close	い-adjective
chikatetsu	ちかてつ	subway	noun
chiketto	チケット	ticket	noun
chikokusuru	ちこくする	to be late	transitive する-verb
chippu	チップ	(computer) chip	noun
chokoreeto	チョコレート	chocolate	noun
chouzou	ちょうぞう	statue	noun
chuui	ちゅうい	attention	noun
chuushoku	ちゅうしょく	lunch	noun

D

Reading	Word	Translation	Word Type
daigakusei	だいがくせい	college student	noun
daisukina	だいすきな	like very much	な-adjective
damena	だめな	no good	な-adjective
dareka	だれか	somebody	noun
dasu	だす	to take out	transitive う-verb
debittokaado	デビットカード	debit card	noun
deeto	デート	date	noun
denki	でんき	light	noun
densha	でんしゃ	train	noun
denwa	でんわ	telephone	noun
deru	でる	to exit; to leave; to answer (the telephone)	intransitive る-verb
doa	ドア	door	noun
doko	どこ	where	noun
doraibaa	ドライバー	driver	noun
doraina	ドライな	dry	な-adjective

D

Reading	Word	Translation	Word Type
doru	ドル	dollar	noun
doushite	どうして	why	adverb

E

Reading	Word	Translation	Word Type
eiga	えいが	movie	noun
eki	えき	(subway) station	noun
en	えん	yen	noun

F

Reading	Word	Translation	Word Type
fukumu	ふくむ	to contain; to include	transitive う-verb
fukuro	ふくろ	bag	noun
fureru	ふれる	to touch	transitive る-verb
furu	ふる	to fall; to precipitate	intransitive う-verb
furutaimu	フルタイム	full time	noun
futoi	ふとい	fat	い-adjective

G

Reading	Word	Translation	Word Type
gakkou	がっこう	school	noun
gakusei	がくせい	student	noun
gatsu	がつ	month	noun suffix
getsuyoubi	げつようび	Monday	noun
gikyoku	ぎきょく	(theatrical) play	noun
gomi	ゴミ	trash	noun
guroobaruna	グローバルな	global	な-adjective

H

Reading	Word	Translation	Word Type
hachi	はち	eight	noun
hada	はだ	skin	noun
hairu	はいる	to enter	intransitive う-verb
hajimaru	はじまる	to start	intransitive う-verb
hajimeru	はじめる	to start	transitive る-verb
hako	はこ	box	noun
haku	はく	to vomit	transitive う-verb
hana	はな	flower	noun
hanashite	はなして	speaker	noun
hanasu	はなす	to speak	transitive う-verb
hanbai	はんばい	sales	noun
hantaisuru	はんたいする	to object	intransitive する-verb
hanzai	はんざい	crime	noun
harau	はらう	to pay	transitive う-verb
hare	はれ	sunny weather	noun
hata	はた	flag	noun
hataraku	はたらく	to work	transitive う-verb
hayai	はやい	fast; quick; early	い-adjective
hayaku	はやく	quickly	adverb
heru	へる	to decrease	intransitive う-verb
heya	へや	room	noun
hikui	ひくい	low; short	い-adjective
hima	ひま	free time	noun
himana	ひまな	free; available	な-adjective
hinkon	ひんこん	poverty	noun
hinode	ひので	sunrise	noun
hiromeru	ひろめる	to broaden; to spread	transitive る-verb
hiru	ひる	noon	noun
hisho	ひしょ	secretary	noun

H			
Reading	Word	Translation	Word Type
hisomeru	ひそめる	to knit (the brows); to frown	transitive る-verb
hito	ひと	person	noun
hitomebore	ひとめぼれ	love at first sight	noun
hitsuyouna	ひつような	necessary	な-adjective
hon	ほん	book	noun
hontouna	ほんとうな	true	な-adjective
horaaeiga	ホラーえいが	horror movie	noun
hoshii	ほしい	want	い-adjective
hosutofamirii	ホストファミリー	host family	noun
houshin	ほうしん	policy	noun
hyaku	ひゃく	one hundred	noun

I			
Reading	Word	Translation	Word Type
ibento	イベント	event	noun
ichiman	いちまん	ten thousand	noun
ie	いえ	house	noun
igirisujin	イギリスじん	British person	noun
ii	いい	good	い-adjective
iku	いく	to go	intransitive う-verb
inu	いぬ	dog	noun
ireru	いれる	to put in	transitive る-verb
iro	いろ	color	noun
iru	いる	to be; to exist	intransitive る-verb
iru	いる	to need	intransitive う-verb
isha	いしゃ	doctor	noun
itsu	いつ	when	noun
iu	いう	to say	transitive う-verb
iyana	いやな	unpleasant	な-adjective

J

Reading	Word	Translation	Word Type
jaketto	ジャケット	jacket	noun
jettokousutaa	ジェットコースター	roller coaster	noun
ji	じ	hour	noun suffix
jibun	じぶん	oneself; myself	noun
jiinzu	ジーンズ	jeans	noun
jikan	じかん	time	noun
jimu	ジム	gym	noun
jishin	じしん	self-confidence	noun
jogingu	ジョギング	jogging	noun
joken	じょけん	advice	noun
joudan	じょうだん	joke	noun
joushi	じょうし	boss	noun
jugyouchuu	じゅぎょうちゅう	while in class	noun
juu	じゅう	one hundred	noun
juugyouin	じゅうぎょういん	employee	noun
juuhachi	じゅうはち	eighteen	noun
juyou	じゅよう	(economic) demand	noun

K

Reading	Word	Translation	Word Type
ka	か	mosquito	noun
kaado	カード	card	noun
kaban	かばん	bag	noun
kaesu	かえす	to return	transitive う-verb
kaiga	かいが	painting	noun
kaigi	かいぎ	meeting	noun
kaisha	かいしゃ	company	noun
kakaku	かかく	price	noun
kakaru	かかる	to cost	intransitive う-verb

Appendix C: Dictionary • 99

K

Reading	Word	Translation	Word Type
kakei	かけい	family lineage	noun
kaku	かく	to write	transitive う-verb
kami	かみ	paper	noun
kanbai	かんばい	sold out	noun
kanjou	かんじょう	feelings	noun
kanojo	かのじょ	she	noun
kanshasuru	かんしゃする	to be grateful	transitive する-verb
kansou	かんそう	dry	noun
karai	からい	spicy	い-adjective
kare	かれ	he	noun
kariru	かりる	to borrow	transitive る-verb
kasa	かさ	umbrella	noun
kau	かう	to buy	transitive う-verb
keeki	ケーキ	cake	noun
keisatsu	けいさつ	police	noun
kenkouna	けんこうな	healthy	な-adjective
ki	き	spirit; heart; mood; tree	noun
kifusuru	きふする	to donate	transitive する-verb
kinbenna	きんべんな	diligent	な-adjective
kinniku	きんにく	muscle	noun
kinou	きのう	yesterday	noun
kireina	きれいな	neat; tidy; clean	な-adjective
kiru	きる	to wear	transitive る-verb
kissaten	きっさてん	coffee shop	noun
kizutsukeru	きずつける	to hurt (one's feelings)	transitive る-verb
kodomo	こども	child	noun
kokka	こっか	national anthem	noun
komedii	コメディー	comedy	noun
konbini	コンビニ	convenience store	noun

K

Reading	Word	Translation	Word Type
konpuuta	コンピュータ	computer	noun
konsaato	コンサート	concert	noun
koohii	コーヒー	coffee	noun
kore	これ	this	noun
koto	こと	thing	noun
kougi	こうぎ	lecture	noun
koujou	こうじょう	factory	noun
koukaisuru	こうかいする	to regret	transitive する-verb
koukoku	こうこく	advertisement	noun
kowai	こわい	scary	い-adjective
kukkii	クッキー	cookie	noun
kumori	くもり	cloudy weather	noun
kurai	くらい	dark	い-adjective
kurasu	クラス	class	noun
kurasumeeto	クラスメート	classmate	noun
kurejittokaado	クレジットカード	credit card	noun
kuru	くる	to come	intransitive irregular verb
kuruma	くるま	car	noun
kyou	きょう	today	noun
kyoukai	きょうかい	church	noun
kyoukasho	きょうかしょ	textbook	noun
kyoutou	きょうとう	Kyoto	noun

M

Reading	Word	Translation	Word Type
machigai	まちがい	error	noun
mai	まい	NA	counter for flat objects such as cookies

M			
Reading	Word	Translation	Word Type
mame	まめ	bean	noun
massugu	まっすぐ	straight (direction)	adverb
matsuri	まつり	festival	noun
mayu	まゆ	eyebrow	noun
meiyo	めいよ	honor	noun
memo	メモ	note	noun
miitingu	ミーティング	meeting	noun
mimi	みみ	ear	noun
miru	みる	to see; to watch	transitive る-verb
mise	みせ	store	noun
mizu	みず	water	noun
mokutekichi	もくてきち	place of destination	noun
mono	もの	thing	noun
moppu	もっぷ	mop	noun
motto	もっと	more	adverb
mushiatsui	むしあつい	humid	い-adjective
mushisuru	むしする	to disregard; to ignore	transitive する-verb
musume	むすめ	daughter	noun
muzukashii	むずかしい	difficult	い-adjective

N			
Reading	Word	Translation	Word Type
nagai	ながい	long	い-adjective
nai	ない	nonexistent	い-adjective
naka	なか	inside	noun
nani	なに	what	noun
narau	ならう	to learn	transitive う-verb

N			
Reading	Word	Translation	Word Type
naru	なる	to become; to sound (a telephone ring)	intransitive う-verb
natsu	なつ	summer	noun
nemui	ねむい	sleepy	い-adjective
nen	ねん	year	noun suffix
neru	ねる	to sleep	intransitive る-verb
nichi	にち	day of the month	noun suffix
nichiyoubi	にちようび	Sunday	noun
nigiyakana	にぎやかな	bustling	な-adjective
nihongo	にほんご	Japanese	noun
nijimu	にじむ	to run (color)	intransitive う-verb
nijuu	にじゅう	20	noun
nikki	にっき	diary	noun
nin	にん	NA	counter for people
ninkina	にんきな	popular	な-adjective
nomu	のむ	to drink	transitive う-verb
noujou	のうじょう	agricultural farm	noun
nusumu	ぬすむ	to steal	transitive う-verb
nuuyookushi	ニューヨークし	New York City	noun

O			
Reading	Word	Translation	Word Type
odoru	おどる	to dance	intransitive う-verb
ofuro	おふろ	bath	noun
oiriina	オイリーな	oily	な-adjective
oishii	おいしい	delicious	い-adjective
okanemochi	おかねもち	rich	noun
okashii	おかしい	funny	い-adjective
okiru	おきる	to wake up	intransitive る-verb

O

Reading	Word	Translation	Word Type
omoi	おもい	heavy	い-adjective
omoshiroi	おもしろい	interesting	い-adjective
omou	おもう	to think	transitive う-verb
onrain	オンライン	online	noun
ooi	おおい	many	い-adjective
ookii	おおきい	large; great	い-adjective
opera	オペラ	opera	noun
oriru	おりる	to get out of (a car)	transitive る-verb
osumousan	おすもうさん	sumo wrestler	noun

P

Reading	Word	Translation	Word Type
paatii	パーティー	party	noun
pakkeeji	パッケージ	package	noun
petto	ペット	pet	noun
piano	ピアノ	piano	noun
piinatsu	ピーナツ	peanut	noun
purejidento	プレジデント	president	noun
purezento	プレゼント	present	noun
purodakuto	プロダクト	product	noun
purodakutodezain	プロダクトデザイン	product design	noun

R

Reading	Word	Translation	Word Type
renshuu	れんしゅう	practice	noun
renshuusuru	れんしゅうする	to practice	transitive する-verb
reshiito	レシート	receipt	noun
resutoran	レストラン	restaurant	noun
rinjin	りんじん	neighbor	noun

R

Reading	Word	Translation	Word Type
ritsu	りつ	rate	noun
ryokousuru	りょこうする	to travel	transitive する-verb
ryou	りょう	quantity; amount	noun
ryoushin	りょうしん	parents	noun

S

Reading	Word	Translation	Word Type
sagaru	さがる	to go down	intransitive う-verb
saifu	さいふ	wallet	noun
samui	さむい	cold	い-adjective
sara	さら	dish	noun
sasayaku	ささやく	to whisper	transitive う-verb
se	せ	height	noun
seetaa	セーター	sweater	noun
seihin	せいひん	product	noun
seijika	せいじか	politician	noun
seikou	せいこう	success	noun
seikousuru	せいこうする	to succeed	intransitive する-verb
sekijuuji	せきじゅうじ	Red Cross	noun
sendensuru	せんでんする	to advertise	transitive する-verb
sensei	せんせい	teacher	noun
serapisuto	セラピスト	therapist	noun
shaberu	しゃべる	to chat	transitive う-verb
shawaa	シャワー	shower	noun
shi	し	city	noun
shichi	しち	seven	noun
shiken	しけん	test	noun
shimin	しみん	citizen	noun
shinkirou	しんきろう	mirage	noun

S

Reading	Word	Translation	Word Type
shiraberu	しらべる	to investigate	transitive る-verb
shiru	しる	to know	transitive う-verb
shitsumon	しつもん	question	noun
shizukana	しずかな	quiet	な-adjective
shoku	しょく	employment	noun
shokuji	しょくじ	meal; diet	noun
shokuryou	しょくりょう	food	noun
shoujikina	しょうじきな	honest	な-adjective
shounen	しょうねん	boy	noun
shounin	しょうにん	witness	noun
shukudai	しゅくだい	homework	noun
sono	その	that	pre-noun adjectival
sore	それ	that	noun
soto	そと	outside	noun
souji	そうじ	cleaning	noun
soujisuru	そうじする	to clean	transitive する-verb
subarashii	すばらしい	splendid; excellent	い-adjective
sukaato	スカート	skirt	noun
sukaipu	スカイプ	Skype	noun
sukejuurusuru	スケジュールする	to schedule	transitive する-verb
sukina	すきな	liked	な-adjective
sukottorandojin	スコットランドじん	Scottish person	noun
sukunai	すくない	scarce; a little	い-adjective
sumimasen	すみません	excuse me	expression
suriraa	スリラー	thriller	noun
suru	する	to do	transitive irregular verb
sushi	すし	sushi	noun
suupaa	スーパー	supermarket	noun

S			
Reading	Word	Translation	Word Type
suupu	スープ	soup	noun
suwaru	すわる	to sit	intransitive う-verb

T			
Reading	Word	Translation	Word Type
taberu	たべる	to eat	transitive る-verb
taihenna	たいへんな	great	な-adjective
takai	たかい	expensive; high; tall	い-adjective
take	たけ	length	noun
tanoshii	たのしい	fun	い-adjective
tashikani	たしかに	certainly	adverb
te	て	hand	noun
teineina	ていねいな	polite	な-adjective
tenisu	テニス	tennis	noun
tenki	てんき	weather	noun
terebi	テレビ	television	noun
tesuto	テスト	test	noun
toire	トイレ	restroom	noun
toki	とき	time	noun
tomeru	とめる	to stop	transitive る-verb
tomodachi	ともだち	friend	noun
toranpu	トランプ	playing cards	noun
toreeningu	トレーニング	training	noun
toshokan	としょかん	library	noun
touchakusuru	とうちゃくする	to arrive	intransitive する-verb
toukyou	とうきょう	Tokyo	noun
tsukareru	つかれる	to get tired	intransitive る-verb
tsukeru	つける	to turn on (a light)	transitive る-verb
tsuku	つく	to tell (a lie)	transitive う-verb

T			
Reading	Word	Translation	Word Type
tsuku	つく	to gain (muscle)	intransitive う-verb
tsukuru	つくる	to manufacture; to make	transitive う-verb
tsurutsuru	つるつる	slippery	noun
tsuzuku	つづく	to continue	intransitive う-verb

U			
Reading	Word	Translation	Word Type
uketoru	うけとる	to accept	transitive う-verb
uketsukegakari	うけつけがかり	receptionist	noun
umai	うまい	skillful	い-adjective
undou	うんどう	exercise	noun
undousuru	うんどうする	to exercise	intransitive する-verb
untenmenkyoshou	うんてんめんきょしょう	driver's license	noun
ureshii	うれしい	glad; happy	い-adjective
urusai	うるさい	loud	い-adjective
ushinau	うしなう	to part with	transitive う-verb
uso	うそ	lie	noun
utau	うたう	to sing	transitive う-verb
utsukushii	うつくしい	beautiful	い-adjective

W			
Reading	Word	Translation	Word Type
wairo	わいろ	bribe	noun
wakamono	わかもの	young person	noun
warau	わらう	to laugh	intransitive う-verb
warui	わるい	bad	い-adjective
wasureru	わすれる	to forget	transitive る-verb

W			
Reading	Word	Translation	Word Type
watashi	わたし	I	noun
watashitachi	わたしたち	we	noun

Y			
Reading	Word	Translation	Word Type
yachin	やちん	rent	noun
yakusha	やくしゃ	actor	noun
yakyuu	やきゅう	baseball	noun
yaru	やる	to do	transitive う-verb
yasai	やさい	vegetable	noun
yasui	やすい	cheap	い-adjective
yomu	よむ	to read	transitive う-verb
yoru	よる	evening; night	noun
yuka	ゆか	floor	noun
yuki	ゆき	snow	noun
yume	ゆめ	dream	noun
yushutsusuru	ゆしゅつする	to export	transitive する-verb
yuubinkyoku	ゆうびんきょく	post office	noun
yuumeijin	ゆうめいじん	celebrity	noun
yuumeina	ゆうめいな	famous	な-adjective
yuusousuru	ゆうそうする	to mail	transitive する-verb
yuutiriti	ユーティリティ	utilities	noun

Z			
Reading	Word	Translation	Word Type
zannenna	ざんねんな	deplorable; disappointing	な-adjective
zou	ぞう	elephant	noun

www.ingramcontent.com/pod-product-compliance
Lightning Source LLC
LaVergne TN
LVHW041630070426
835507LV00008B/539